KINGDOM THEOLOGY

Kingdom Theology

Inaugurated Eschatology and Its Implication for Missions

G. CARLTON MOORE JR.

WIPF & STOCK · Eugene, Oregon

KINGDOM THEOLOGY
Inaugurated Eschatology and Its Implication for Missions

Copyright © 2024 G. Carlton Moore Jr. All rights reserved. Except for brief quotations in critical publications or reviews, no part of this book may be reproduced in any manner without prior written permission from the publisher. Write: Permissions, Wipf and Stock Publishers, 199 W. 8th Ave., Suite 3, Eugene, OR 97401.

Wipf & Stock
An Imprint of Wipf and Stock Publishers
199 W. 8th Ave., Suite 3
Eugene, OR 97401

www.wipfandstock.com

PAPERBACK ISBN: 979-8-3852-1124-1
HARDCOVER ISBN: 979-8-3852-1125-8
EBOOK ISBN: 979-8-3852-1126-5

06/17/24

Unless otherwise indicated, Scripture quotations are from The Holy Bible, English Standard Version®, copyright ©2001 by Crossway, a publishing ministry of Good News Publishers. All rights reserved.

For my wife Rhonda, the one who supports and encourages me to never give up and to see my manuscript through

Contents

Acknowledgments | ix

Introduction | xi

CHAPTER 1
KINGDOM OF GOD | 1

    Christological | 3
        Political Kingdom | 3
        Providential Kingdom | 7
        Redemptive Kingdom | 13
    Eschatological | 15
        Hermeneutical Link between Protology and Eschatology | 15
        Eschatological Purpose of the Kingdom of God | 16
        Eschatological Realm and Reign of the Kingdom of God | 18
            Realm | 18
            Reign | 21
    Kingdom of God Defined | 27

CHAPTER 2
INAUGURATED ESCHATOLOGY AND THE TWO-AGES MODEL | 32

Inaugurated Eschatology and the Two-Ages Model | 32
    The Two-Ages Model | 33
        Biblical Evidence of the Two-Ages Model | 36
            The Implications of the Two-Ages Model | 43
    Inaugurated Eschatology | 44
        The Sign of the Eschaton: The Resurrection | 47
            The Resurrection and New Creation | 48
            The Kingdom of God and New Creation | 52

The Sign of the Eschaton: The Descent of the Holy Spirit on the Church | 59
    Christ as the End-Time Temple | 59
    The Church as the End-Time Temple | 61
    The Eschatological Genesis of the End-Time Temple | 66
    The Church as the End-Time Manifestation of the Reign of God | 71
Conclusion | 72

CHAPTER 3

PRACTICAL IMPLICATIONS: MISSION OF THE CHURCH | 78

Mission of the Church | 78
    Models For Missions | 79
        The Holistic Model | 79
            The Traditional View | 81
            The Ecumenical View | 81
            The Via Media | 82
    Critique Of The Holistic Model | 87
        The Missional Model | 90
    Critique Of The Missional Model | 94
        The Mission of the Church | 95
            What Is Mission? | 97
            Great Commission Proof Texts | 98
            Conclusion | 106
    The Inaugurated Kingdom And Its Implication For The Church | 107
        The First Adamic State of the Cultural Mandate | 108
        The Second Adamic State of the Cultural Mandate | 119
            Mission Accomplished | 121
            Believers' Share In Christ's Accomplishment | 123
Conclusion | 125

CHAPTER 4

SUMMARY, CONCLUSION, AND REFLECTIONS SUMMARY | 128

    Reflections | 130

Bibliography | 143

Author Index | 151

Scripture Index | 155

Acknowledgments

I wish to record my deep sense of gratitude and profound thanks to my doctoral defense committee members at Reformed Presbyterian Theological Seminary in Pittsburgh, PA: Dr. Richard Gamble, professor of systematic theology; Dr. Jeffrey Stivason, professor of New Testament studies; and research advisor and program director Dr. C. J. Williams, professor of Old Testament studies. I want to thank them for their keen and clarifying insight, guidance, and encouragement with this project during all stages to bring this thesis to fruition.

Introduction

Both kingdom theology, in general, and eschatology, in particular, form and inform both the reality and our perspective of missions. But throughout church history there have been multivalent models of conceptualization, making it "one of the most debated and varied concepts in the history of Christian thought."[1] Case in point is the futuristic concept of the kingdom of God by proponents of dispensational premillennialism. Dispensationalists have associated the kingdom of God with the future return of Jesus Christ and the end of human history, making eschatology a too narrowly defined doctrine, too narrowly defined by the Parousia and a terrestrial millennial reign.[2] With such a narrow view, the accent has been futuristic, making eschatology the "last chapter" of what God will do in the world and in the church. The "forces of culture" and the irreducible complexity[3] of the kingdom of God symbol play no small of a role in this. As Stephen Stookey says,

> History points to one certainty with regard to doctrinal definitions of the kingdom of God: models of the kingdom will change. While the overarching motifs of kingdom thought reoccur throughout history—future hope, present spiritual reality, political rule, ecclesiastical rule, societal transformation—new conceptions of the old emerge. The forces of culture combined with the tensions in biblical kingdom language continue to generate proposed models

---

1. Stookey, "Models of the Kingdom," 38.

2. Taylor, "Early Christian's Expectations," 32. Taylor is a case in point; his notion of a terrestrial kingdom puts the focus of the kingdom of God and eschatology on the future.

3. If at the molecular level cells are "irreducibly complex," then by analogy it should be no surprise to us that kingdom of God too is irreducibly complex to a greater degree. See Behe, *Darwin's Black Box*.

of the kingdom of God, and so it will be as Christians seek to understand their present mission and their future reality.[4]

Christians in every generation have had to grapple with a persistent and perpetual question: since Christ's kingdom is "not of this world," yet his church is "in this world," what then is the church's calling? My hope is to offer a biblically based and theologically coherent model for the kingdom of God motif for the purpose of helping Christians (individually and corporately) to navigate the missional landscape in our understanding of the nature and scope of her calling, namely missions, in relation to the spirituality of the church.[5] I hope to contribute by connecting the dots not only by associating the theoretical aspect of eschatology to practical ministry, but also associating eschatology to the life of the church, namely missions. If inaugurated eschatology is true, then eschatology currently forms and informs not only the "structure" of New Testament eschatology, according to Vos, but also missions today. This is the positive contribution. However, there is a need too regarding the focus of missions. What eschatological approach one uses will affect one's understanding of the nature and practice of missions. Mission creep, that is to say the expansion of the church's original objective(s), is a real concern for the contemporary church that undermines the spiritual nature of the church; how one understands both the notion of the kingdom of God, in general, and eschatology, in particular, affect one's focus on missions. Case in point: if one holds to a transformative approach to culture in the same vein of a theonomic or a classic postmillenarian attempt to Christianize culture, then how one goes about missions, including

---

4. Stookey, "Models of the Kingdom," 52.

5. What I am arguing for in today's twenty-first-century church was a hallmark doctrine of Old School Presbyterianism of the nineteenth century: that is the doctrine of the spirituality of the church over and against the New School accent on social change/reform. See Hart and Muether, *Seeking a Better Country*, 141–43, 161, 173, 178, 180, 194, 223, 226–27, 231–38. As Alan Strange observes regarding Charles Hodge's doctrine of the Old School spirituality of the church, " . . . the spirituality of the church . . . means that the church is the Spirit-composed communion of saints, who dwell in a variety of particular churches across the earth, who are called to a specific task, the gathering and the perfecting of the saints. It is to that task and not to mere ritualism ecclesiastically or politics civilly that this true church is called." Strange, *Doctrine of the Spirituality of the Church*, 174. The doctrine of the spirituality is not pietistic. Just as with Hodge's nuanced use of the doctrine, holding to the doctrine of the spirituality of the church does not preclude the church's prophetic voice from addressing matters in political communities and civil societies, like the sin of man stealing and chattel slavery in the nineteenth century or the sin of homosexual marriage or so-called civil unions in the twenty-first century. . .

Introduction

the allocations of resources, will be different from a non-transformative approach to culture by way of an amillennial understanding that does not seek to Christianize culture, but focuses on making disciples. This applies also to the current social justice debate among evangelicals, in general, and those in the Reformed tradition, in particular.

In the first chapter, the kingdom of God is broadly defined using christological and eschatological categories. First, the kingdom of God is christological. Christologically, the kingdom of God is defined over and against, and distinct from, notions of the kingdom of God as political/earthly and the kingdom of God as providential. The former kingdom is Christ-less; the latter kingdom is, generally speaking, one domain of Christ's kingdom. In contradistinction, the kingdom of God is specifically christological in that Christ is king and redeemer who institutes the new covenant of grace, a covenant that formally administers said kingdom of God. Second, the kingdom of God is essentially eschatological. That is to say, both the principle notion and purpose of the kingdom of God are eschatological in that the covenant of grace is eschatological. God instituted the covenant of grace to ultimately realize the new eschatological creation, not only in the "already" or present eschatology, but also in the "not yet" or future eschatology, where the people of God, and all of creation, will experience glorification. In short, the kingdom of God is the eschatological reign of God in Christ, manifested in this age and the age to come!

In the second chapter, the present reality of the kingdom of God in this age is emphasized. God's reign is victorious in Christ Jesus, in his church in history, and in this present age not only in principle but in reality, that is to say, in its inaugurated form. First, I will argue that God's reign is a reality in this present age as the inaugurated kingdom of new creation. Second, God's reign in this present evil age is a victorious reign. Third, God's reign in this present evil age is reigning victoriously in his church militant. Believers who overcome—that is, those who overcome in victory on earth by patiently enduring tribulation without compromise—ironically are overcome by the world too in an earthly defeat. In short, this is how we are to understand both God's victorious reign within history and God's victorious reign within sacred history through his church.

And in the third chapter, we will look at how the reign of Christ affects the nature and our notion of missions. An inaugurated notion of the kingdom of God in Christ serves as a theological foundation and model of orientation for ministry. This inaugurated notion of the kingdom of God

Introduction

not only forms and informs the "structure" of New Testament eschatology, according to Vos, but also practical issues regarding the church's notion of mission. How one understands both the definition of kingdom of God, in general, and eschatological, in particular, has many practical implications for ministry. In this chapter, I will be addressing the practical implications of the inaugurated notion of the kingdom of God regarding the mission of the church. As stated above, mission creep is a real concern for the contemporary church. Navigating the missional landscape without losing our purpose is a must. My driving question is: what are the implications for mission (under the mandate of the Great Commission)?

In short, my thesis is that since both the inauguration of the kingdom of God's new creation is an "already" current reality in this present age, and the consummation of the kingdom of God's new creation is a "not yet" future inevitability for the age to come—both being a work of God and God alone that will be demonstrated—and since the message (that is, the gospel) of the inauguration of the kingdom of God's new creation is something the mission of God's people are mandated to witness, proclaim, and pronounce to the world, then the mission of God's people is very narrow and specific, which will also be demonstrated. If we fail to make this crucial distinction, the church's mission will lose its biblical emphasis on gospel proclamation through word and sacrament, church planting (and strengthening), and costly discipleship. In short, if we fail to do this, we will be relinquishing and abdicating and abandoning our most singular and particular and peculiar kingdom-of-God vocation: that is, the harvesting and the gathering and the perfecting of the saints. The doctrine of the spirituality of the church in our day must never be compromised.

CHAPTER 1

KINGDOM OF GOD

WHAT IS THE KINGDOM OF GOD?[1] Bolt contends that the notion of the kingdom of God is multivalent, susceptible to many values, meanings, and interpretations. Bolt bemoans the fact that the notion of the kingdom of God has been used as a ". . . normative lodestar . . . in modern thought to advance an eschatology that is in tune with a progressive social ethic—building the kingdom on earth."[2] Case in point: Bolt points to how the symbol of the kingdom of God has been misused as a rallying cry against the institution of the church. Quoting Alfred Loisy, who said, "Jesus proclaimed the kingdom of God, and what came was the church," Bolt says that such a sentiment has served to put a wedge between the kingdom of God and the church. He says,

> [This approach] serves as the measuring stick for this sentiment: say no to the church; say yes to the kingdom. The kingdom is larger than the church; the kingdom propels us out into the world; the kingdom directs us to the work of God everywhere. That is frequently the direction taken by those who push "the gospel of the kingdom" over against what they judge to be narrow understandings of Christian salvation that are only [sic] individual and personal.[3]

---

1. Bolt, "Just What Do You Mean," 259.
2. Bolt, "Just What Do You Mean," 259.
3. Bolt, "Just What Do You Mean," 261.

Because of the "misuse" of the kingdom of God symbol, Bolt says, "it is perhaps prudent to avoid using [it] as the cornerstone of a Christian social vision."[4]

Is Bolt correct? Should we avoid using the kingdom of God motif to form and inform our vision of society, culture, and missions? If he's correct, would not the kingdom of God motif, by default, be relegated to "narrow understandings of Christian salvation that are only individual and personal"? In this chapter, I will argue that not only should we not avoid using the kingdom of God motif but that the biblical perspicuity of the nature of the kingdom of God demands our use, in spite of its misuse and abuse!

How should the kingdom of God be conceptualized, that is, the arrival, continuation, and final consummation as it relates to biblical eschatology? George Ladd too says that the kingdom of God has a "bewildering diversity of explanations."[5] Nonetheless Ladd sees a clear biblical explanation: "Since the historical mission of Jesus is viewed in the New Testament as a fulfillment of the Old Testament promise, the entire message of the kingdom of God embodied in Jesus' deeds and words can be included in the category of eschatology?"[6] We first notice in Ladd's understanding of the kingdom of God that it's inherently christological, that the kingdom of God and its message is about Jesus: what Jesus said, what Jesus did, and (implied by Ladd) who Jesus is. The person, work, and message of Jesus—including his fulfillment of Old Testament promises that pointed to the coming of God's kingdom—embody the kingdom of God.[7] Second, we notice that the kingdom of God consists of the category of eschatology.[8] The kingdom of God is constitutive of both Christology and eschatology. How one understands

---

4. Bolt, "Just What Do You Mean," 282. He also adds that neo-Kuyperians must also "refrain from making claims such as the following: the church is essentially 'a redeemed humanity restored to its original task assigned to mankind at the beginning,' and the missionary mandate of Matthew 28 is basically a republication or restatement of the cultural mandate of Genesis. No, it is not."

5. Ladd, *Gospel of the Kingdom*, 14.

6. Ladd, *Presence of the Future*, 325–26.

7. Hoekema, *Bible and the Future*, 41–43.

8. Moltmann, *Theology of Hope*, 16. Moltmann's *Theology of Hope* is a theology of culture in relating the Christian faith and the secular world. Though his method is not a method of correlation, according to Tillich, he still seems to give epistemic primacy to the questions raised by secular society than to the answers provided by Scripture, letting society set the agenda by default. However, I overall agree with his conviction that eschatology forms and informs all of the Christian faith. See also Erickson, *Contemporary Options in Eschatology*, 44–51.

eschatology will form and inform one's notion of the kingdom of God. These are two very important considerations that will be expanded upon throughout this project; suffice to say, the kingdom of God motif is both christological and eschatological.

CHRISTOLOGICAL

First, in what sense is the kingdom of God christological?[9] Thomas Watson, that great Puritan divine, distinguishes clearly the multivalent physiognomy regarding the kingdom of God. He asks: what is the meaning of the kingdom of God in the New Testament as it pertains to Christ? He states:

> Let us show what it does mean. (1) He [i.e., Jesus] does not mean a political or earthly kingdom. The apostles indeed did desire Christ's temporal reign. 'Wilt thou at this time restore the kingdom again to Israel?' Acts i 6. But Christ said his kingdom was not of this world. John xviii 36. So that when Christ taught his disciples to pray, 'Thy kingdom come,' he did not mean it of any earthly kingdom, that he should reign here in outward pomp and splendour. (2) it is not meant of God's providential kingdom. 'His kingdom ruleth over all;' that is, the kingdom of his providence. Psa. ciii 19. This kingdom we do not pray for when we say, 'Thy kingdom come;' for this kingdom is already come. God exercises the kingdom of his providence in the world. . . . What kingdom then is meant when we say, 'Thy kingdom come'? Positively as twofold kingdom is meant. (1) The kingdom of grace. . . . (2) We pray also, that the kingdom of glory may hasten . . .[10]

Political Kingdom

First, Watson references the kingdom of God as a political or earthly kingdom that Jesus' contemporaries (including not only Second Temple

---

9. See Goldsworthy, *Gospel and Kingdom*, 47–49. Goldsworthy posits three hermeneutical presuppositions: (1) Redemptive history is progressive. (2) Redemptive history is incomplete without the authoritative interpretation of the New Testament. (3) Redemptive history is interpreted in light of the New Testament's teachings of Christ. For further study on the progressive character of the kingdom of God and the history of redemption, see VanGemeren, *Progress of Redemption*; Swain, *Trinity, Revelation, and Reading*, 23.

10. Watson, *Lord's Prayer*, 59.

Kingdom Theology

Judaism, but also his own disciples) came to expect, but that Jesus unequivocally and categorically rejects by simply saying that his kingdom is not of this world, that is to say, such a kingdom of this world is inherently a Christless kingdom. Ridderbos is helpful in understanding this development of the kingdom of God as an earthly kingdom. Ridderbos contends that the kingdom of God/heaven in Second Temple Judaism indicates the coming of God's dominion to liberate Israel from the yoke of bondage from the heathen nations and to subject the nations to God.[11] Ridderbos says that though the coming of the kingdom was far from unanimous in Second Temple Judaism's pseudepigraphic and apocryphal writings, there was a parallel thread, a parallel warp and woof of, on one hand, the restoration of the people of Israel and the house of David, and on the other hand, an ". . . emphasis on the supernatural-transcendent character of the great time of salvation."[12] These parallel, orthogonal lines seem to converge at the vanishing point of Second Temple Judaism's notion of nationalism. Nationalism has been called by scholars of Second Temple Judaism the "third pillar" of foundational beliefs that define Judaism of both the past and present. This foundationalism is known as the "conventional" or "normative" view of Judaism.[13] The three pillars of the conventional view posited are: monotheism, revelation (or Torah), and the nation of Israel—that is, the binding national election of Israel as the people of God, the people of God as different from all the peoples (or nations) of the world. The upshot is that the ethnic Jew is secure in the knowledge that redemption is assured for the nation in general, and the individual who is a member of that nation. As Schechter says:

> Judaism . . . combines two widely differing elements, and when they are brought out separately, the aspect of the whole is not taken sufficiently into account. Religion and [sic] race form an inseparable whole of Judaism. The Jewish people stand in the same relation to Judaism as the body to the soul. . . . The central point of Jewish theology and the key to an understanding of the nature of Judaism is the doctrine, "God chose Israel as His people."[14]

Even Dunn, who is averse to normative approaches as such, speaks of a "unifying core" within Judaism. The core includes: monotheism, election,

11. Ridderbos, *Coming of the Kingdom*, 9.
12. Ridderbos, *Coming of the Kingdom*, 10.
13. Moore, *Judaism in the First Centuries*, 125–32.
14. Schechter, *Some Aspects of Rabbinic Theology*, xvii–xviii.

covenant/law, and land/temple. He says, "These then can be fairly described as the four pillars on which the Judaism(s) of Jesus' time was/(were) built, the axiomatic convictions around which the more diverse interpretations and practices of the different groups within Judaism revolved." He says that ". . . the conviction that Israel is God's elect, chosen by God, and God's vineyard is absolutely axiomatic" [15]

How do we define nationalism in this context? Elliot says, "A nationalistic theology could . . . consist, at one and the same time, of the hope that God would save Israel (theological ideals) by means of a national campaign (military ideals) that would result in political independence (political ideals)."[16] This view of nationalism or nationalistic theology formed and informed the notion of the political kingdom that Jesus' disciples were still looking for and that Jesus categorically and unequivocally rejected as a Christless kingdom.

Before I move on to address Watson's second notion of the kingdom of God as a providential kingdom, let me say more about the notion of the kingdom of God as an earthly kingdom. The expectation of the kingdom of God as an earthly kingdom didn't end with Second Temple Judaism. The kingdom of God as an earthly kingdom not only can be formed and informed by theological/political constructs such as nationalism according to Second Temple Judaism, but can also be formed and informed by sociological constructs. Case in point is H. Richard Niebuhr's classic work.[17] Goerner says, "Niebuhr modestly expresses the hope that this work may serve as a 'stepping stone' to some future writer who may present a complete story of Christianity as the progressive embodiment in human society of a great spiritual ideal."[18] For Niebuhr, the kingdom of God is a great spiritual ideal and dynamism progressively embodied in human society. What does Niebuhr mean by this? For Niebuhr, the idea of the kingdom of God "has been the dominant idea in American Christianity." In colonial times, it meant the "sovereignty of God"; in times of the Great Awakening and revivals and nineteenth-century optimism, it meant the "reign of Christ," and in relatively recent times it has come to mean the "kingdom on earth."[19] These three related motifs regarding the expression of the kingdom

---

15. Dunn, *Parting of the Ways*, 18–35.
16. Elliot, *Survivors of Israel*, 34.
17. Niebuhr, *Kingdom of God in America*, xii.
18. Goerner, "Kingdom of God in America," 134.
19. Niebuhr, *Kingdom of God in America*, xii.

of God are distinctively protestant visions as opposed to the Roman Catholic understanding; the former emphasizes the *visio Dei*, the latter the *regnum Dei*.[20] Medieval Roman Catholicism identified the kingdom of God with the church, instantiated in her hierarchical institution. Protestantism, says Niebuhr, nurtured social ferment and political movements and change in no small part by characterizing the kingdom of God in terms of God's primacy, immediacy, and closeness. Niebuhr says, "Medieval Catholicism with its spiritualizing doctrine of the coming kingdom represents the adjustment of the Christian faith to the long postponement of Christ's return and redemption of his promise." He says, by contrast, that "the new movement [that is, Protestantism] was impatient not only with the systems of mediators of divine rule and grace, but also with the deferment of life's promise. Its word was 'now.'"[21] Protestantism, as a social movement, is more than a movement of protest, for Niebuhr, but also "construction," that is to say, a "turn from protest and conflict to construction" in the American context of Protestant Christianity.[22] Niebuhr's notion of the kingdom of God in the American context is not instantiated in static institutions (as with the Catholic Church), but instantiated in dynamic movements and causes that are critical, vibrant, revolutionary, and (even at times) sectarian.[23]

I want to make a comment before I proceed to Watson's second observation. Niebuhr's motifs and concomitant moral, social visions are, as we can see, themselves inherently sociological, that is, inherently earthly, as was Walter Rauschenbusch's "socialist vision" of the kingdom of God. It's worth noting that the nationalism of Second Temple Judaism (which sought a Messiah without a cross) is very much like what Niebuhr critiques regarding American religiosity; that is, in the American context, Second Temple Judaism's notion of nationalism has been transposed into a modern register where the motif of the reign of Christ degenerates from a voluntary society of missions and denominations into competing rivals between said societies, which ". . . [seeks] the extension of democratic institutions

---

20. Niebuhr, *Kingdom of God in America*, 18.
21. Niebuhr, *Kingdom of God in America*, 25–26.
22. Niebuhr, *Kingdom of God in America*, 43.
23. It must be kept in mind that Niebuhr is employing Troeltschian sociological categories taught by his teacher, i.e., Troeltsch's church-sect typology within sociology of religion. Niebuhr bemoaned the deterioration of the three kingdom motifs with their concomitant moral visions for society. For further insight into this and the dynamism involved in the wake of today's culture wars, see Goldstein, "Dialectics of Religious Conflict," 77–78.

[both political and ecclesiastical institutions]—of necessity by recourse to military force—in order that all the world might share in the blessing of the [sic] kingdom of God on earth."[24] Suffice it to say, any political or earthly notion of the kingdom of God (whether in the nationalist context of Second Temple Judaism or in the sociological context of modern American religiosity) degrades into a Christless kingdom.

Providential Kingdom

Second, Watson refers to the kingdom of God as a providential kingdom. Watson notes that the kingdom of God as providence is distinct from the coming kingdom of God. The kingdom of God as a providential kingdom, also known as the "essential kingdom,"[25] is the kingdom where God the Father, God the Son, and God the Holy Spirit rule and reign by inherent right and original right, inherent and original in the sense that the Son of God as the agent of creation has always ruled and reigned without investiture and/or conferral. The eternal Son of God is the sovereign Lord over all creation, who not only created but providentially sustains creation. In this sense, Christ as the eternal Son of God is king over his providential kingdom. Unlike the earthly or political kingdom rejected by our Lord, Christ's kingdom (as both the eternal Son of God and as the incarnate God-Man[26]) includes the providential kingdom in a general way. What do I mean? VanDrunen[27] is helpful at this point when he says,

---

24. Niebuhr, *Kingdom of God in America*, 183–84.

25. Symington, *Messiah the Prince*, 27, 144–45.

26. More will be said below about Christ as God's mediatorial vicegerency and rule over the domain of the providential kingdom.

27. Though I am sympathetic and have learned much from the insight of VanDrunen's two-kingdoms perspective (as I also have from theonomists and their perspectives regarding the application of the law), I am not a modern "Escondido" two-kingdoms advocate. I am not an advocate (unlike VanDrunen), because I believe and reason that the moral law does and/or should in fact have bearing on the political, civil, and moral landscape of our society. A Christian magistrate not only should prudently deliberate and judge, then act and decide on issues at hand based on the natural law (as VanDrunen advocates), but should also engage issues regarding statecraft based on his conscience, a conscience formed and informed by the revealed will of God in Scripture. Case in point: a Christian lawmaker should advocate against gay marriages/civil unions, while upholding the biblical definition of marriage between one man and one woman as Scripture clearly teaches as a creation ordinance. The same goes, *mutatis mutandis*, for other Christians in their various vocations. Christian ministers should also prophetically

> By "the Reformed two kingdoms doctrine," I refer to the idea that God in his Son rules all things, but rules them in a twofold way. On the one hand, God, as Creator and Sustainer, rules the natural and social orders, even using ordinary human institutions such as the State as instruments of his reign. On the other hand, God, as redeemer in Christ, bestows salvation upon a chosen people, whom he rules unto everlasting life through the ministry of his church. The two kingdoms, therefore, correspond to this twofold divine rule. The terminology used in Reformed theology to name these two kingdoms was not fixed. John Calvin . . . used the terms "civil" and "spiritual," respectively. Many later Reformed theologians referred to the "kingdom of power" and "kingdom of grace." In my own recent writing and teaching I have come to prefer the terms "common" and the "redemptive."[28]

VanDrunen's "common" kingdom is Watson's "providential" kingdom. Just as Watson noticed two distinct kingdoms, likewise the Reformed two-kingdoms proponents see two distinct kingdoms that must not be mixed or confused as one kingdom or separated or divided as two radically distinct kingdoms; this is due to the fact that Christ rules both as mediator in a twofold manner and mode.

---

advocate for this, as well as to call our nation to repent and turn to God, an advocacy that is part of mandate of the Great Commission to disciple the nations. Though there is an institutional separation of church and state, there is no separation of God and state.

28. VanDrunen, "Reformed Two Kingdoms Doctrine," 178. My point in introducing Reformed/radical two kingdoms is not to argue for a Reformed two-kingdoms doctrine and/or a social ethic and its implications for cultural engagement. I am arguing for the doctrine of the spirituality of the church, not the Reformed two-kingdoms view as noted in my footnote above. My point here is to show that what Thomas Watson sees and understands is the same as what VanDrunen is here seeing and understanding by his terminology, that is to say that there is a providential kingdom of God (what VanDrunen call a "common kingdom"), where God in his Son rules and reigns the world, and that this providential kingdom is not the same as the kingdom of grace and kingdom of glory (what VanDrunen calls a "redemptive kingdom") that Watson expounds upon in his sermon on the Lord's Prayer. Both Watson and VanDrunen agree that there is a twofold manner of God's rule, a twofold divine rule; one is a natural/social order, the other a redemptive/ecclesial order. Instead of the nomenclature of "two kingdoms," which can imply separation and division, one can just as easily call it a "twofold divine dominion" under one King and kingdom, which is one kingdom over two distinct domains, which I prefer. However as one conceptualizes it, this twofold dominion must maintain an identity without either mixture or confusion, separation or division. Apart from the social implications of "transformative" vs. "non-transformative" approaches to culture, neo-Calvinists and R2K thinkers have more in common than not.

Both Christians and non-Christians, redeemed and unredeemed, are citizens or subjects within Christ's providential kingdom. As David says, "The Lord has established his throne in the heavens, and his kingdom rules over all" (Ps 103:19). David appeals to both the nature/origin and scope of God's providential kingdom. David sees God's providential kingdom established in the transcended nature of God, that is, "his throne in the heavens"; and the scope of that rule and reign is universal, that is, "rules over all." How does God in Christ exercise his rule over the providential kingdom according to Scripture (for example in Heb 1:3)? This providential kingdom is formally ratified and administered under the rubric of "common grace" as distinct from "special grace" by means of the postdiluvian covenant of Noah.[29] VanDrunen says,

> By the covenant of common grace I refer to God's covenant with Noah after the flood, recorded in Genesis 8:20–9:17. Three characteristics of this covenant identify it as a covenant of common grace (and thus distinct from the covenant of grace) and also addresses the issue left unanswered at the end of the previous subsection, namely, how we are to understand the human cultural vocation after the fall (since Adam's cultural mandate, per se, does not apply).[30]

---

29. Though I consider the Noahic covenant to be a covenant of common grace, there is a strong case as well that said covenant is a covenant of redemptive grace. It is a matter of fact that the Noahic covenant falls within and plays a part in redemptive history. In what way(s) does said covenant play a part in redemptive history? First, Noah was a type of Christ. He was a type of the second Adam, a typical redeemer. Everyone on the ark with Noah was saved from the judgement of God, a judgment in which 1 Peter prototypically connects with eschatological judgment. Second, after the waters receded Noah and his family stepped onto and into a new world, a world symbolically cleansed by the water judgment. This symbolically cleansed world is a type of the "new heavens and the new earth." Third, Noah was commanded to take seven clean and two unclean animals onto the ark. The distinction between clean and unclean animals will become the basis of Israel's sacrificial system, which was typical of Christ's work of redemption. Lastly, the redemptive seed promised in Genesis 3:15 continues through Noah and his son, Shem. God's mandate against murder helped to providentially preserve said redemptive seed from extermination, preserving the hope of redemption. These examples strongly demonstrate and make a strong case that the Noahic covenant is essentially one of grace, not common grace. For further insight into the place of redemption the Noahic covenant plays, see Chalmers, "Importance of the Noahic Covenant."

30. VanDrunen, "Reformed Two Kingdoms Doctrine," 183.

Kingdom Theology

Before I elaborate on these three characteristics, is VanDrunen correct in recognizing the Noahic *covenant* being a covenant of common grace[31] and not an administration of a covenant of grace, that the providential kingdom is formally administered by means of the Noahic covenant? Vos contends that revelation, immediately after the flood, progresses around the notion and "development of life." He says,

> What is ordained by God and the promise made have equal reference to the entire Noachian family. But we know that the work of redemption was carried on in the line of Shem *only*; the arrangement made is not even confined to the human race; it is made with every living creature, nay, with the earth herself; that the *berith* is a *berith* of nature appears from the *berith*-sign; the rainbow is a phenomenon of nature, and absolutely universal in its reference. All the signs connected with redemption are bloody, sacramentally dividing signs.[32]

First, Vos observes that the line of Seth, and Seth alone (emphasized by my italicizing of only), is the story and work of redemption carried onward; second, not only the entire family of Noah, but also the entire human race, the entirety of all living creatures, along with the earth itself is covered by the Noahic covenant; third, the sign of the covenant does not have the typical sacramental characteristic: namely, the rainbow; the rainbow is neither a bloody sign nor a dividing sign, dividing the redeemed from the unredeemed, making the sign a "phenomenon of nature." Contrary to the Noahic covenant being a formal ratification and administration of the covenant of grace, Vos compellingly observes that the Noahic covenant is a ratification and administration of the covenant of common grace.

Herman Bavinck also makes a similar observation.[33] He notes that in the antidiluvian age, both common and special grace "... flow[ed] in a single

---

31. Common grace refers to God's benevolence to all people regardless of spiritual condition. The Noahic covenant is God's covenant of common grace with the earth, despite mankind's depravity, to sustain its order until the consummation. God's definitive, eschatological judgment is held in abeyance until Christ's return. This covenant of common grace is common to all. Common grace is the universal provision of God for all mankind according to the covenant made with Noah as the representative of the whole of mankind and the whole of the natural world. The universal provision is what Watson correctly observes as being the providential kingdom.

32. Vos, *Biblical Theology*, 51.

33. Bavinck, *Reformed Dogmatics*, 3:218–19. Kuyper also observes that the Noahic covenant is a covenant of common grace that "... seeks to make the church possible and to secure a place of rest for the church, but it does not involve the church as such. This

channel."[34] However, with Noah, a new era unfolds in that the common grace that "... manifested itself immediately after the fall now exerted itself more forcefully in the restraint of evil."[35] The covenant that God—made with his creation so as to restrain evil in a postdiluvian age, in order not to backslide into an unrestrained prediluvian condition— formalized and administered in the Noahic covenant is a common grace covenant. This covenant, "though rooted in God's [special] grace . . . because it sustains and prepares for it, is not identical with it."[36] What kind of pledge is the Noahic covenant? Bavinck says,

> It is rather a "covenant of long-suffering" made with God with all humans and even with all creatures. It limits the curse on the earth; it checks nature and curbs its destructive powers; the awesome violence of water is reined in; a regular alternation of seasons is introduced. The whole of the irrational world of nature is subjected to ordinances that are anchored in God's covenant.[37]

For Bavinck, it's worth noting that he rejects two extremes: on one end of the extreme, he rejects conflating the covenant of grace and the covenant of nature or common grace instantiated in the Noahic covenant. For Bavinck these are not to be mixed or confused; they are not identical. The Noahic covenant is not a covenant of special grace; however, on the other end, both are also not to be radically separated or divided because both the covenants of common and special or redemptive grace entail an involvement of nature.

Herman Witsius observes the same thing when he says that the Noahic covenant "was not formally and precisely the covenant of grace." For Witsius there is no mention of a ". . . spiritual and saving benefit . . . to all men."[38] Witsius does observe that we are not to deny that the covenant of grace is not implied, that is to say that ". . . the promises of it were also sealed to believers by the rainbow."[39] Quoting Rivet, he sees in Revelation

---

covenant involves man as man, man in his society on earth with other men, man in relation to the animals, and man in his relationship to the destructive elements of nature." See Kuyper, *Common Grace*, 1:13.

34. Bavinck, *Reformed Dogmatics*, 216.
35. Bavinck, *Reformed Dogmatics*, 218.
36. Bavinck, *Reformed Dogmatics*, 218.
37. Bavinck, *Reformed Dogmatics*, 218. That is, providence is anchored in God's Noahic covenant of common grace.
38. Witsius, *Economy of the Covenants*, 2:239.
39. Witsius, *Economy of the Covenants*, 2:241.

4:3 that "Christ therefore appears crowned with a rainbow, as the messenger of grace and peace."[40] His point is that since Christ has reconciled the Father with believers, believers do not have to be afraid of the "deluge of divine wrath" on the day of the Lord. In short, the sign of the rainbow is analogically (not univocally) a symbol of grace and peace for God's people, but this analogical application does not negate the nature of the Noahic covenant being a formal ratification and administration of the covenant of common grace.

In short, VanDrunen says, ". . . God has made with human beings in the post-fall world, a covenant of common grace, by which God providentially maintains this world and all human beings in it . . ."[41] The providential kingdom is formally administered by means of the Noahic covenant.[42] This covenant is a covenant of nature and common grace, not a supernatural pledge of special, saving grace. This covenant, which corresponds to the providential kingdom, is the means by which God through Christ, the God-man, exercises his providential rule for the good of his bride, the church. How do we characterize the providential kingdom in contradistinction to what is meant by the New Testament's notion of the kingdom of God as it pertains uniquely to Christ and the Lord's Prayer? VanDrunen is helpful. He observes:

> A first characteristic of this Noahic covenant is that it is universal. Literally nothing in all creation is left out of this covenant. Its provisions extend to the "ground" or "earth" (Gen 8:21; 9:13) and to the very cosmic forces of nature ("seedtime and harvest, cold and heat, summer and winter, day and night"—8:22). It includes not only every subsequent human being ("I [God] will establish my covenant with you [Noah] and your offspring after you"—9:9) but even "every living creature of all flesh" (9:10,15,16,17).[43]

In contradistinction to the covenant of grace—which is not universal but particular—the covenant of common grace, which corresponds to the providential kingdom, is universal. Second, VanDrunen also notes that not only is the covenant of common grace universal, it's also preservative,

---

40. Witsius, *Economy of the Covenants*, 2:241.

41. VanDrunen, "Reformed Two Kingdoms," 183.

42. VanDrunen does superb work tracing the Noahic origins of both political communities, in general, and civil government, in particular, in both the Old and New Testaments. See VanDrunen, *Politics after Christendom*, 79–123.

43. VanDrunen, "Reformed Two Kingdoms," 183.

non-transformative, non-redemptive. The covenant of common grace in light of the second and civil use of the law restrains man's sinfulness; it does not redeem man from sin. VanDrunen argues that God pledges not only to restrain evil, but also to restrain himself from destroying this postdiluvian age with water again, that "... the covenant with Noah only promises to preserve the world and the human race from the worst effects of sin and to maintain some measure of order in the cosmos and in human society. ... God offers no promise to forgive sin or to bring an eschatological new creation."[44] Third, the covenant of common grace has an expiration date. It's not permanent. It will come to an end. As VanDrunen writes, "... [God] promises the blessings of preservation 'while the earth remains' (8:22). A time is coming when the earth will no longer remain, but while it does this covenant will not fail."[45] More will be said later, but the common grace covenant formally ratified and administered by the Noahic covenant will come to an end with "this present evil age" in light of "the age to come." In conclusion, Watson is correct to refer to the kingdom of God as a providential kingdom, a kingdom distinct from the coming kingdom of God. As VanDrunen says, "... the Noahic covenant is God's means for administering his reign in the common kingdom." Unlike the earthly kingdom, which is Christless, the providential kingdom is not only trinitarian, but also christological—in that all rule and authority and dominion and power in this present age and the age to come has been given to Christ as the God-man according to Ephesians 1:21–23.

Redemptive Kingdom

However, there is a third (and principal) notion of the kingdom of God, a notion that's distinct from both an earthly kingdom and the providential kingdom. This principal notion of the kingdom of God is the kingdom that is a dominant and prominent motif in the New Testament. As noted, Watson calls this principal kingdom a "twofold kingdom" of grace and glory.[46] How does God administer this principal twofold kingdom? Just as the providential kingdom is formally administered by the covenant of common grace, likewise this principal twofold kingdom is administered

---

44. VanDrunen, "Reformed Two Kingdoms," 184.
45. VanDrunen, "Reformed Two Kingdoms," 184.
46. Watson, *Lord's Prayer*, 59.

Kingdom Theology

by the covenant of grace.[47] The covenant of grace is God's means of administering his principal twofold kingdom of redemption. Christ's twofold kingdom, a kingdom that is formally administered by the covenant of grace, is not for preservation but for transformation[48] and redemption and consummation.[49]

What characterizes this covenant of grace? First, it is always particular in contradiction to the covenant of common grace, which is universal. An example of this is seen in the Abrahamic covenant.[50] This particular redemption, administered by means of the Abrahamic covenant of grace, was for a part of the human race, not the whole of the human race. In the Abrahamic administration of grace it was only Abraham's household. Also, particular redemption, administered by means of the Mosaic covenant, was only for one nation, that is to say, the nation of Israel, not the gentile nations. In these last days, particular redemption is administered by means of the new covenant of grace with the New Testament church extending to the whole world, that is to say, the nations of the world, not to every single person in the world, a sort of ethnic universalism.

Second, the covenant of grace is always transformative (Rom 12:2) and redemptive in contradiction to the covenant of common grace, which is preservative, short of salvation. Unlike the promise of the providential kingdom administered by the covenant of common grace, a promise to preserve this world from the effects of sin—the redemptive kingdom by means of God's vicegerent provides a redemptive solution to the problem of sin. That solution is ultimate salvation from sin, from the power of the

---

47. For an overview of the relationship between the covenant of grace and the kingdom of God, see Baugh, *Majesty on High*, 105–35; Gentry and Wellum, *Kingdom through Covenant*:; Rhodes, *Covenants Made Simple*; Robertson, *Christ of the Covenants*.

48. What I mean by transformation is in the eschatological sense of the new creational age to come in Romans 12:2. Our cultural endeavors in light of our Christian vocations can never truly be "transformational."

49. Graeme Goldsworthy suggests that we look at Scripture (especially the Old Testament) as a history of redemption. This sacred narratological approach emphasizes God as the main character in redeeming for himself a people. The accent is on God, not the people of God. If God is the main narratological character in redemption, then what is the goal of redemption? The goal of redemption is reestablishing or reinstating the kingdom of God. This is why it's apropos to describe the principal kingdom of God as redemptive. See Goldsworthy, *Gospel and Kingdom*, 46.

50. The first instance of the covenant of grace is in Genesis 3:15. More will be said below.

devil,[51] and transformative re-creation of the heavens and earth. Common grace preserves nature, while redemptive grace consummates nature. The means of saving justification is faith in God's promises (for example, Gen 15:6; cf. Gal 3:11; Rom 4). The root of justification is the crucifixion of Christ by means of the new covenant where the shed blood of Christ was formally ratified and administered by the new covenant (for example, Luke 22:20) and typologically foreshadowed by the multitude of prototypical sacraments in the Mosaic covenant of the Christ to come.

ESCHATOLOGICAL

In short, the redemptive kingdom of God motif—in contradistinction to both notions of an earthly and providential kingdoms—is thoroughly and uniquely christological in a particular, redemptive, transformative sense. However, there is (as Ladd contends) a second motif: eschatological.[52] The redemptive kingdom of God is eschatological in contrast to the covenant of common grace, which is protological. Below I will ask pertinent questions to flesh out the eschatological physiognomy of God's eschatological kingdom. First, what is the link between protology and eschatology? Second, what is the eschatological purpose of the kingdom of God? Third, what is the principal nature of the kingdom of God?

Hermeneutical Link between Protology and Eschatology

What is the connection between protology and eschatology?[53] Creation is inextricably linked to new creation.[54] The kingdom of God is eschatological in the sense that it has been inaugurated at creation, culminating eschatologically with Christ, uniting "all things in him, things in heaven and things on earth" (Eph 1:10). This is clear from the beginning to the end of salvation history, bracketed by Genesis and Revelation:

---

51. Bock, "Wheat and the Weeds," 38. Bock says, "The kingdom does not eradicate evil immediately, but it still makes a claim on all until the time of consummation. The kingdom is not merely arriving in the world, it is invading it and is in the process of manifesting itself across the whole of the creation, whether one accepts it or not."

52. Beale defines eschatology ". . . as the 'already-not yet new creational reign in Christ.'" Beale, *New Testament Biblical Theology*, 177.

53. See Gage, *Gospel of Genesis*.

54. VanGemeren, *Progress of Redemption*, 460.

Kingdom Theology

> In the beginning, God created the heavens and the earth. (Gen 1:1)

> Then I saw a new heaven and a new earth, for the first heaven and the first earth had passed away, and the sea was no more. And I saw the holy city, new Jerusalem, coming down out of heaven from God, prepared as a bride adorned for her husband. And I heard a loud voice from the throne saying, "Behold, the dwelling place of God is with man. He will dwell with them, and they will be his people, and God himself will be with them as their God. And he who was seated on the throne said, Behold, I am making all things new. (Rev 21:1–3)

Kenneth Matthews argues that "in the beginning" can also mean inauguration. If true, then "in the beginning" (namely, inauguration) presupposes (by definition) an end. This eschatological prolepsis is by definition not "an end," but "the end" in relationship to "the beginning."[55] Narratologically speaking, the kingdom of God is the metanarrative of redemption from the beginning to the end. VanGemeren says,

> The Bible begins with the account of creation (Gen. 1–2) and ends with a description of a more glorious creation (Rev. 21–22). [The kingdom of God] is the organic development whereby God works out his plan for the redemption of a new humanity from all the nations (Rev. 5:9; 7:9). Creation, in a real sense, is the preamble to the history of redemption.[56]

In short, Genesis 1–2, which inaugurated creation, is inextricably linked with Revelation 21–22, which consummates creation, that is, new creation. Both Genesis and Revelation bracket the entirety of salvation history, which is the narrative of the kingdom of God. This inextricable link between old creation and new creation is the ground for both continuity (a rejection of annihilation) and discontinuity (a rejection of utopianism). Yet, the discontinuity between old and new creation will be greater than said continuity.

Eschatological Purpose of the Kingdom of God

What is the eschatological purpose of the kingdom of God? The principal notion or purpose of the kingdom of God is eschatological in that the

---

55. Mathews, *Genesis 1—11:26*, 126–27.
56. VanGemeren, *Progress of Redemption*, 40.

Kingdom of God

covenant of grace is eschatological. God instituted the covenant of grace to ultimately—not penultimately, as with the providential kingdom by means of the covenant of common grace—realize the new eschatological creation, not only in "the already" or present eschatology (Watson's notion of the spiritual kingdom of grace), but also in the "not yet" or future eschatology, where the people of God and all of creation will experience glorification, that is to say, Watson's notion of the consummate kingdom of glory.[57] VanDrunen sums these notions up this way where he says,

> It is proper, I suggest, to recognize this covenant of grace as the means by which God administers the redemptive kingdom. God not only rules the whole world through his general providence, but also has established Christ as the special king of his redeemed people. Through this covenant, God in Christ bestows the blessings of salvation on them, gathers them into a worshiping community, makes them citizens even now of his heavenly city, and will at last bring them into everlasting residency in that new creation.[58]

In other words, the metanarrative of the kingdom of God is a story that gives the covenant people of God an outlook, an outlook where Christ will fulfill all and bring all things to a consummated, eschatological end. This gives us hope, eschatological hope. Jürgen Moltmann says:

> From first to last, and not merely in the epilogue, Christianity is eschatology, is hope, forward looking and forward moving, and therefore also revolutionizing and transforming the present. The eschatological is not one element of Christianity, but it is the medium of the Christian faith as such, the key in which everything else in it is set.[59]

In short, the purpose of history[60] is the sovereign plan of God to unite all things again under one domain, one kingdom—namely, to unite all things in Christ and to put all things under his feet (Eph 1:22). The meta-purpose is to reinstate and reestablish the eschatological, theocratic kingdom of God in Christ, where both cult (sacred) and culture (the profane) are integrated as one.

---

57. More will be said below regarding the eschatological notion of present and future eschatology, and the two-ages model.

58. VanDrunen, "Reformed Two Kingdoms," 185.

59. Moltmann, *Theology of Hope*, 16.

60. For a concise explication of the three views of history—i.e., ancient, atheistic, and Christian—see Hoekema, *Bible and the Future*, 24–33.

Eschatological Realm and Reign of the Kingdom of God

My last question is: what is the principal nature of God's kingdom? Is the kingdom of God a place or power or both? Ridderbos says that the kingdom of God does have a spatial connotation to it; he writes:

> There is no doubt that the former sense [i.e., rule or reign of power] . . . is the most prominent usage of the word [*basileia*] in various central pronouncements about the "kingdom of heaven" in the gospels. The spatial meaning of kingdom is then a secondary one. When the text says that the *basileia ton ouranon* "is at hand" . . . we should not in the first place think of a special or static entity, which is descending from heaven; but rather of the divine kingly rule actually and effectively starting its operation; therefore, we should think of the Divine action of the king. . . . The kingdom of heaven preached by John and Jesus is first of all a process of a dynamic character. . . . For the coming of the kingdom is the initial stage of the great drama of the history of the end.[61]

Realm

First, before I speak on the non-spatial rule of the kingdom of God, let me address the spatial component of the kingdom. What are the spatial connotations? Originally speaking, the location of the kingdom of God was in Eden. The garden-temple was the spatial location of the kingdom of God, where both cult and culture were integrated under theocratic rule and realm, dominion and domain. Both Adam and Eve were in the presence of God. Adam, as the federal head of humanity along with his posterity, was commanded, under the covenant of works, to exercise dominion over the prelapsarian order of creation, to fill the earth with their offspring in light of the dominion mandate. What is this mandate?

> The first phrase, "be fruitful and multiply," means to develop the social world: build families, churches, schools, cities, governments, laws. The second phrase, "subdue the earth," means to harness the natural world: plant crops, build bridges, design computers, and compose music. This passage is sometimes called the Cultural

---

61. Ridderbos, *Coming of the Kingdom*, 92. Also see Ladd, "Kingdom of God," 233. Cf., e.g., Col 1:13; Matt 11:11; Luke 7:28; Luke 16:16; Matt 21:31; 23:13; Luke 11:52. Ladd sees a "present realm," a spiritual realm of light vs. darkness.

> Mandate because this passage tells us that our original purpose was to create cultures, build civilizations—nothing less.[62]

More will be said below on the creation/cultural mandate in my fourth chapter, but Pearcey's description is correct (though anachronistic) in pointing to both the social and natural dimensions of the original mandate. Just as the garden-temple had both a social and a natural dimension, likewise the rest of creation was to have a social and natural dimension subsumed and sublimated by Eden as the borders of Eden were to be enlarged in light of the original cultural mandate. Alexander says,

> An increasing population would create a city around the temple. Throughout time, the whole earth would become a holy garden-city. While Genesis 2 merely introduces the start of this process, the long-term outcome is the establishment of an arboreal temple-city where God and humanity coexist in perfect harmony.[63]

Eden was the original culturally mandated building location where humanity, under the federal head of Adam, was to exercise said theocratic dominion and accordingly extend, enlarge, and expand the cultural borders of kingdom of God located in Eden. Revelation alludes to the finished work of expanding Eden. The metaphor for this finished work is a city, a finished city of God where the city inhabitants are from every tribe and language and people and nations, where "death shall be no more, neither shall there be mourning nor crying nor pain anymore, for the former things have passed away" (Rev 21:4; 5:9).[64] The spatial dimension of the kingdom begins at creation and culminates with the design of the new creation, a new heavens and earth (with "heavens and earth" being a biblical merism for all of creation, including space and time[65]), where and when the kingdom of our Lord and Savior Jesus Christ will rule and reign forever and ever (Rev

---

62. Pearcey, *Total Truth*, 50. More will be said below regarding the cultural mandate.
63. Alexander, *From Eden to the New Jerusalem*, 25–26.
64. Alexander, *From Eden to the New Jerusalem*, 14.
65. Ladd, *Theology of the New Testament*, 47. Ladd notes that in both ages—i.e., this present age and the age to come—creatures will always live in both space and time. Eternity in the age to come will not be timeless eternity (only God transcends time and is timeless), but unending time. Ladd writes, "In biblical thought eternity is unending time. In Hellenism men longed for release from the cycle of time in a timeless world beyond, but in biblical thought time is the sphere of human existence both now and in the future. The impression given by the American Standard Version in Revelation 10:6, 'that there should be time no longer,' is corrected in the Revised Standard Version, 'there should be no more delay.'"

22:4–5; 11:15). Though the spatial dimensions of the kingdom of God are alike—that is, Eden is a location; new creation is a location—however, there is a dissimilarity in that the latter is greater that the former. VanGemeren notes that, "[the history of redemption] does not begin with a high point only to end up with the new earth as an equally high point. The new creation is better than the first because it will be perfect, holy, and characterized by the presence of God the Father and the Lord Jesus Christ (Revelation 21:22)."[66]

This is what, in part, is new about the new creation vs. the old; that is, the former is a qualitative and quantitative accelerated advancement as the result of the gospel through the person and work of Christ. The new creation is qualitatively better in that it is the glorification of creation, unlike the garden of Eden, which was not in a state of glorification as demonstrated, in part, by Adam's mandate to "to work it and keep it" (Gen 2:15).[67] This also applies, *mutatis mutandis*, to the promised land. Frame notes,

> The Promised Land was intended as a type, a picture, a first installment of a greater inheritance to come. Today the promise of the land takes a new form: the promise of the new heavens and new earth. It is not that the Promise of Canaan has been abrogated. It is rather seen a part of a larger promise, which Abraham's descendants by faith all inherit.[68]

Also, it is important to note that this spatial notion, in one sense, applies to the entire world in this present age as the stage of redemption. In Matthew 13 the unconverted are spatially (not spiritually and morally) viewed as within Christ's kingdom until the end of the age. It reads, "The Son of Man will send forth His angels, and they will gather out of His kingdom all stumbling blocks, and those who commit lawlessness" (Matt 13:41). The main point of Jesus' parable is that in this world (in general) and in the visible church (in particular)—both being the stage in which God's kingdom is played out—will be an admixture of counterfeit Christians with genuine Christians. In what sense is this world the stage of redemption? Simply put, this world is a historical stage in the drama of redemption. If the reader will recall, this historical stage is this present age, an age administered by the

---

66. VanGemeren, *Progress of Redemption*, 64.

67. This is not to say that there will be no work per se in the new heavens and earth. However, the work is qualitatively different (there will be no sense of improvement), and there will be no need to "keep" or guard the new creation from sin.

68. Frame, *Escondido Theology*, 182.

Kingdom of God

Noahic covenant of common grace. As Bavinck notes, this covenant is "... rooted in God's [special] grace ... because it sustains and prepares for it, [though it] is not identical with it."[69]

Reign

Second, although the kingdom of God exhibits creational aspects, aspects of both space and time, nonetheless the principal notion of the kingdom of God exhibits most forcefully the impression of the "... right to rule, the actual energetic forth-putting of God's royal power in acts of salvation."[70] George Ladd correctly contends that "[a]s one surveys the literature ... he would be led to conclude that the prevailing consensus is that the kingdom of God is God's effective reign or rule to be established over the world."[71] Reign, not realm, is the primary and fundamental meaning of the biblical concept of kingdom.[72] The proper metaphor is a throne, not real estate. The psalmist correlates the kingdom of God with the throne of God: "The Lord has established His throne in the heavens; and his kingdom rules over all" (Ps 103:19).[73]

Not only does the biblical metaphor of God's throne fittingly capture the notion of kingdom, but so does the theological language of "transcendence." John Frame recognizes that God's transcendence has a spatial connotation to it in the sense that God is "above" creation. But this gives the impression that God's otherness is a spatial category. But Frame contends that God is not located in some place beyond creation. Frame says,

> That may be part of the thrust of the terms 'Most High,' 'exalted,' and 'lifted up,' but there must be more to it. . . . We should . . . see these expressions primarily as describing God's royal dignity. . . . The expressions of transcendence refer to God's rule, his kingship, his lordship.[74]

---

69. Bavinck, *Reformed Dogmatics*, 218

70. Vos, *Teaching of Jesus*, 31. Also see Gray, *Biblical Doctrine*, 20–25; Chilton, "Kingdom of God," esp. 273–74.

71. Ladd, "Kingdom of God," 230.

72. Much of the literature evinces this. See, e.g., Ladd, *Jesus and the Kingdom*, 126; Beasley-Murray, *Jesus and the Kingdom*, 74.

73. Many other texts comport with this observation. See, e.g., Ps 145:11–13.

74. Frame, *Doctrine of the Knowledge*, 15.

Kingdom Theology

Ridderbos says the reign of God is an assertion of his right to rule. He says that the kingdom of God is dominated by a "theocratic point of view," a view that asserts a "theocentric proclamation" that is a "kingly assertion" over his creation. Ridderbos says that

> The idea of the kingdom of God is more comprehensive exactly because it is not only oriented to the redemption of God's people, but to the self-assertion of God in all his works. Not only does he place Israel, but also the heathen nations, the world, and even the whole of creation, in the wide perspective of the realization of all God's rights and promises.[75]

This theocratic notion[76] of the kingdom, defined as God's self-assertion, reveals God's majesty, power, and might to rule and reign![77] God's kingdom is constitutive of "God's own actions," which are based on God's self-asserting activity.[78] Because of this, the kingdom of God has a "strongly dynamic connotation."[79] The kingdom of God is inextricably connected with the personhood of God, as represented in God's vicegerent, that is, the Christ as man.[80] Regarding the kingdom of God motif, ". . . Jesus proclaimed not a geographical sovereignty or an ethical advance caused by human submission to God; it is the rule or dynamic reign of God, the earthly exercise of his sovereignty."[81] This exercise of God's sovereignty is a reinstatement of human vicegerency; as McCartney says, "The arrival of

---

75. Ridderbos, *Coming of the Kingdom*, 23.

76. Meredith Kline says that theocracy is simply God's reign (holy dominion) coming through or being manifested though his holy realm (holy domain). Kline rightly argues that God's theocratic kingdom is not the kingdom of men nor is it the providential kingdom. God's theocratic kingdom is a *sui generis* institution established by God himself, not erected by men. As Kline says, "The peculiar kind of kingdom established in Eden at the beginning (and later redemptively renewed) differs radically from other kinds of world kingdoms that arose after the Fall. Whatever analogies exist between the theocracy and the other kingdoms, however many falsely proclaimed theocracies there may be, there is only one genuine theocratic kingdom under the special rule of the living God." Kline, *Kingdom*, 49.

77. Ridderbos, *Coming of the Kingdom*, 19.

78. Ridderbos, *Coming of the Kingdom*, 24.

79. Ridderbos, *Coming of the Kingdom*, 24–25.

80. McCartney, "Ecce Homo." More will be said below regarding Christ's mediatorial reign as vicegerent.

81. McCartney, "Ecce Homo," 1. The geographical sovereignty (i.e., theocratic domain) will come about with the consummation of the kingdom. The inauguration of the kingdom entails a theocratic dominion.

the reign of God is the reinstatement of the originally intended divine order for earth, with [sic] man properly situated as God's vicegerent."[82] In fact this is by definition what the eschatological kingdom of God is; it is the restoration of God's kingdom first proclaimed in Genesis 3:15, where God says, "I will put enmity between you and the woman, and between your offspring and her offspring; he shall bruise your head, and you shall bruise his heel." This has been called the "mother promise."[83] This promise is the warp and woof that runs throughout the Old Testament. The seed of the woman will bruise the serpent's head; this prediction promises the coming redeemer. This promise is the "first gospel" or promise that God's reign will be reinstated by the seed of the woman, that the Christ will bruise the head of the serpent by means of his death.[84] This so-called *protoevangelium* telegraphs God's plans to restore his kingdom by redeeming his people by the coming Messiah-King. This coming redeemer is predicted to be a man; later he is predicted to be a Hebrew (Gen 22:18); and further along in salvation history from the tribe of Judah (Gen 49:10); and even later a human king from the line of David (2 Sam 7:12–14)—evincing a narrowing of the promised redeemer who will reinstate God's eschatological reign.[85]

George Ladd adds that within the culture milieu of Second Temple Judaism the kingdom of God, as an eschatological reign or rule, was a fact. He says, "The rabbinic teaching about the kingdom of God as the reign or rule of God is as much a fact of history and an element in Jesus' religious

---

82. McCartney, "Ecce Homo," 2. McCartney notes in footnote 5 that this "reinstatement of the original prelapsarian order" goes beyond the original order or original kingdom; "it's an advancement over the Adamic state." "This prelapsarian order was the original establishment of the kingdom of God under the administration of the Covenant of Work, (as the Standards teach) . . . wherein life was promised to Adam; and in him to his posterity, upon condition of perfect and personal obedience." See, e.g., Westminster Confession of Faith 7.2.

83. Hoekema, *Bible and the Future*, 5.

84. Swain, *Trinity, Revelation, and Reading*, 21.

85. Frame, *Salvation Belongs to the Lord*, 119. Frame notes some very important implications. He writes, "First, we should see ourselves as covenant breakers in Adam (Isa. 24:5). In him we have failed the test of works, and we have no hope of ever saving ourselves by our works. But where we failed, in Adam, Christ gloriously succeeded. He obeyed God perfectly and laid down his life as a sacrifice to make up for our disobedience. In ourselves, we are covenant breaker, but in Christ covenant keepers. By thinking about the Covenant of Works, we can learn today that God demands a perfection we cannot attain, that Jesus achieved that perfection, and that in him our salvation is complete. Jesus did everything the Father asked on our behalf. So, nothing can separate us from him or from the Father."

environment as the apocalyptic writings."[86] Ladd argues that even Rudolph Bultmann "recognizes a difference between Jesus and the apocalyptists in that while Jesus proclaimed the imminent apocalyptic event, he had no interest in the content of the event, but only in the fact itself that God would rule."[87] Ladd concludes by saying that the primary notion of the inauguration of kingdom of God is God's reign or rule, not realm and/or age. He says that the

> ... kingdom of God is God's reign and not the new age; and at this point, a clear analogy is found with rabbinic thought. The nobleman who went into a far country to obtain a "kingdom" sought authority to reign as king, that is, kingship (Luke 19:12, 15). Jesus' "kingdom" which is not of this world is the measure of authority resident in him, his kingship (John 18:3). The prayer of the dying thief to be remembered when Jesus comes "in his kingdom" refers to the hope that Jesus, now dying as a criminal, will one day show himself to possess the authority and power of a king (Luke 23:42). ... The prayer for the coming of God's kingdom (Matt 6 10) undoubtedly refers to the eschatological event, but it is a petition for a divine act which has its parallel in the Jewish prayer, "May he set up his kingdom in your lifetime and in your days." It is a prayer for the act of God which will establish the eschatological order. Again, the kingdom which must be received like a child (Mark 10 15; Luke 18 17) is not a realm, present or future, but God's reign.[88]

What's the point of God's reign? Dodd sums it up well. It is "to make the doing of His will the supreme aim." [89] This explains the correlation between the kingdom of God and the message of repentance and submission. Ladd contends that in rabbinic thought the kingdom of God (that is to say, heaven) is always the dynamic notion of reign, not realm, with two aspects to his rule: a provisional rule and a prevailing rule. Regarding the former, in this present age, God manifests his reign through Torah. When men submit themselves in obedience to God's law, then men will experience the kingdom of God's reign. In this sense God's reign is provisional, a reign contingent on men acknowledging God and submitting to him and his law. This rabbinic notion of God's reign acknowledges that a large portion of the world (Jesus' broad way modified and applied to the visible church) is

---

86. Ladd, "Kingdom of God," 233.
87. Ladd, "Kingdom of God," 234.
88. Ladd, "Kingdom of God," 235.
89. Dodd, *Parables of the Kingdom*, 106, 197.

not obeying and acknowledging the reign of God. However, God will not allow this state of affairs to go on indefinitely. On the day of the Lord, God will act to assert his universal kingdom that will "prevail," where God will be King over not only submissive Israel, but also both the acquiescent and rebellious nations as both judge and savior.[90]

Ladd argues that Jesus' notion of God's prevailing and provisional reign follows this pattern with some modification. One modification is the inextricable link between God's reign and order. Ladd says that "when God acts to establish his effective reign in the world, the resulting order is also called the kingdom of God. Basileia can have two eschatological meanings: 'the eschatological act of God and the eschatological order created by God's act.'"[91] Biblical evidence for both regarding the kingdom-reign (that is, *Herrschaft Gottes*) and its concomitant order— that is, the kingdom-reign necessarily ushering in a kingdom-order of justice or a rightly ordered society—is manifold.[92]

However, Jesus' second modification is more significant, setting Jesus apart from other rabbis. Ladd explains,

90. Ladd, "Kingdom of God," 236.

91. Ladd, "Kingdom of God," 237.

92. See, e.g., 2 Chr 20:30; Dan 1:20; 9:1; 11:2; 2 Chr 36:22; Ezra 1:1; Neh 9:35; Esth 1:14, 20; 3:6, 8. For a programmatic and scholarly analysis regarding justice as order vs. justice as inherent rights, see also Wolterstorff, *Justice*. Wolterstorff argues that particular rights are primarily subjective, rather objective. The latter's locus of conceptualization centers around objective order, i.e., "justice as right order." The former revolves around the idea of subjectivity: "justice as inherent rights," i.e., rights that inhere within humans as humans. Basically, he argues that there are only two ways to understand primary justice: justice as right order or justice as inherent rights. Wolterstorff makes a convincing counternarrative argument over and against the secular regime's grand narrative. Contrary to the secular grand narrative—a narrative that recounts the story of the origins of justice as inherent rights as a product of either nominalism or the Enlightenment—Wolterstorff advances another story. He makes the case that justice as inherent rights is not the product of the Enlightenment or even a product of nominalism, but ultimately a product of the biblical Judeo-Christian tradition, that is, both the Old and New Testaments; right order derives ultimately from God's inherent right of worship and obedience, which is transposed in men as inherent rights by virtue of the Imago Dei. In short, by acknowledging the inherent rights of God (first table of the law) and the inherent (inherent as in natural and not social) rights of men bestowed by God (second table of the law)— then this acknowledgment consequently gives rise to justice as a rightly ordered society. Wolterstorff's argument exposes the weakness of the secular regime's narrative (secular protagonists) and anti-secular regime's narrative (communitarians who are the antagonists of rights). Wolterstorff's argument nullifies the intellectual mainstream's argument, wrenching the moral discourse of justice as inherent rights from the exclusive purview of secularists and those who dismiss rights in favor of justice as right order instead.

Kingdom Theology

> Before the eschatological manifestation there was a manifestation of a different sort. God, who would act at the end of history to transform history, had invaded history in the person and mission of Jesus to bring his reign and rule to men. Such a conclusion best explains many gospel sayings. "If it is by the Spirit of God that I cast out demons, then the kingdom of God has come upon you" (Matt 12:28).... God's kingdom is present in Jesus in a new and unique way. In the mission of Jesus, God has taken the initiative. God has acted. God has manifested his kingly rule. The exorcism of demons is indeed a sign of the kingdom, but it is not a sign of an imminent approaching kingdom; rather it is a sign of a present kingdom. In the coming of Jesus, God has entered into history in his kingly activity to accomplish his redemptive purpose.[93]

Contrary to rabbinic teaching that posited that God's reign was present by means of obedience to Torah, Jesus taught that God's reign was present in his person and mission, which is the gospel.[94] Contrary to the apocalyptic thought regarding this age, where God was a remote God (*Deus absconditus*), no longer active in human history, Jesus revealed a new element about God, new regarding his person and work. Ladd says,

> God has once again become dynamically active in history. The Jewish scholar, Montefiore, recognizes this unique factor. "The greatness and originality" of Jesus "opened a new chapter in men's attitude towards sin and sinners" because he sought out sinners rather than avoiding them. The seeking God, the God who is not content to wait for men to turn to him but who searches for the lost, the God who has again become active in history for man's salvation — this is the corollary of the God who has become dynamically active in his kingly rule in Jesus to bring men into the blessings of his rule.[95]

---

93. Ladd, "Kingdom of God," 236–37.

94. For further study regarding the connection between the kingdom of God and the gospel, see Ladd, *Gospel of the Kingdom*. Ladd describes the manifestation of the kingdom (in terms of the resurrection of the dead and the defeat of Satan) as a three-stage rather than a two-stage affair, thereby expressing his belief in chiliasm; it is the three stages constitutive of the Church Age, the eternal state with an intermediate stage in between.

95. Ladd, "Kingdom of God," 238.

KINGDOM OF GOD DEFINED

In light of both Christology and eschatology, how do we now define the kingdom of God? In summary, the expression "kingdom of God" is not found in the Old Testament. However, the expression is most prominent and important in the New Testament.[96] This does not mean that the notion of the kingdom of God is foreign to the Old Testament as the expectation of Yahweh revealing himself "as king in full glory." This notion is a "dominant element" found in both the Major and Minor Prophets.[97] Along with this dominant element is also the concomitant notion of Messiah-King. The notion of both the kingdom of God and the Messiah are inextricably related. Ridderbos says,

> [The kingdom of God] is often unaccompanied by any mention of the Messiah-King. But the one cannot be separated from the other, because what is said about the coming reign of God has no other reach than that of the prophecies about the messianic kingdom of peace.... In short, all that which holds for the coming divine manifestation of the king, also holds for the rule of the Messiah-King. This is to say that it is the Lord, who will again assert his rule over Israel and maintain his kingship over the whole world in and through the coming Messiah-King ... the Redeemer-King of David's house.[98]

Not only is the kingdom of God a dominant concept, but so also is the notion of the Lord as King.[99] God rules his covenant people as a suzerain Lord/King.[100] As covenant Lord/King, God protects and defends, and offers justice and mercy as he rules his people through the administration of his covenant, making Lord/King the dominant image for God.[101]

---

96. Schreiner, *New Testament Theology*, 41.

97. Ridderbos, *Coming of the Kingdom*, 4.

98. Ridderbos, *Coming of the Kingdom*, 6.

99. Frame, *Doctrine of the Knowledge*, 369. Frame argues that "King" and "Lord" are synonyms.

100. The phrase "image of God" is not only an ontological and/or ethical category, but also a political category. That is to say, the concept of royalty is expressed by the Imago Dei. This is based on ancient Near Eastern cultures. The phrase "image of God" was linked to kings. Earthly kings were incarnate images of God. Adam was given regal status to rule as God's vicegerent. See Alexander, *From Eden to the New Jerusalem*, 7. Also, for an extensive discussion of the Imago Dei, ranging for older to contemporary notions, see Kilner, *Dignity and Destiny*.

101. Frame, *Doctrine of the Knowledge*, 367. John Frame suggests "King" for the

Kingdom Theology

Both concepts of God, as King and Lord, terminate in the coming of Christ. Therefore, the kingdom of God is christocentric, contrary to the liberal theological tradition.[102] As Vos says,

> To him the kingdom exists there, where not merely God is supreme, for that is true at all times and under all circumstances, but where God supernaturally carries through his supremacy against all opposing powers and brings men to the willing recognition of the same.[103]

Graeme Goldsworthy contends that there is a pattern to salvation history, a "pattern of the kingdom" from the beginning to the end as "God's people in God's place under God's rule."[104] This pattern terminates in the person of Christ.

In short, how do we define the kingdom of God? The kingdom of God—contrary to the political kingdom and distinct from the providential kingdom—is the redemptive and transformative reign of God. This redemptive and transformative reign is a twofold kingdom of grace and glory. The redemptive and transformative reign of God is formally administered by the covenant of grace. Just as the providential kingdom is formally administered by the covenant of common grace, likewise this principal twofold kingdom of grace and glory is formally administered by the covenant of grace. In the Westminster Confession the covenant of grace is defined by the divines as

---

dominant image for God.

102. For a very helpful and accessible synopsis of modern liberalism's unbiblical conceptualization of the kingdom of God, see Hoekema, *Bible and the Future*, 288–316. Case in point: A. Ritschl and A. von Harnack described the kingdom of God as a human endeavor, making their notion of the kingdom of God kingless. A. Schweitzer, on the other hand, was a corrective over and against the moralism of nineteenth century's cultural Christianity. Schweitzer argued for a "consistent eschatology," meaning that the thrust of Jesus' teaching on the kingdom was not moralistic or immanent, but eschatological, in the sense that Jesus was preoccupied with the future reign of God when God breaks into this age. Jesus expected the imminent end of the world in his lifetime. But alas, Jesus was mistaken and became disillusioned. C. H. Dodd rejected both notions. He reasoned that the kingdom was real on earth in the presence of Jesus, a view known as "realized eschatology." Dodd argued that the eschaton has entered history, the hidden rule of God had been revealed, and the age to come has come. But the fatal mistake with Dodd was that he rejected the notion of a literal second coming of Christ.

103. Vos, *Teaching of Jesus*, 50.

104. Goldsworthy, *Gospel and Kingdom*, 53–54.

> Man, by his fall, having made himself incapable of life by that covenant, the Lord was pleased to make a second, commonly called the Covenant of Grace; wherein He freely offers unto sinners life and salvation by Jesus Christ; requiring of them faith in Him, that they may be saved, and promising to give unto all those that are ordained unto eternal life His Holy Spirit, to make them willing, and able to believe.[105]

This covenant of grace is one covenant, administered throughout redemptive history through different modes of administration. Yet, the substance of the different modes of administration is the same throughout the different dispensation of salvation history, that is, the substance of grace. The covenant of grace was promised in Genesis 3:15 with Adam, instated with Abraham in Genesis 12, expanded through the proto-typical theocratic kingdom of God of the Mosaic covenant—that is, by means of the mode of administration promised through types, ceremonies, and sacrifices—and the Davidic covenant, finding fulfillment in the new covenant and anti-typical kingdom of Christ Jesus, a covenant that did not replace[106] the old covenant, but fulfilled it.[107] Because the redemptive reign of God is administered by the covenant of grace—administered progressively and incrementally throughout salvation history—this reign of God is dynamic, not static through Jesus Christ.[108] The purpose of God's reign in Christ is to redeem God's people from sin, redeem God's people from demonic powers,[109] and finally to establish the new heavens and new earth (cosmic regeneration). The kingdom of God is not merely the reign of God in the hearts of his people (kingdom of grace) but also the reign of God over the entire cosmos. This is the goal of history.[110] In short, the kingdom of God is both a present historical reality and a future historical inevitability. As Ladd says,

---

105. Westminster Confession of Faith 7.3

106. Scofield, *Rightly Dividing the Word*, 23–27. Classical dispensationalism in the vein of Scofield encourages replacement that leads to a radical discontinuity because (as classical dispensationalists see it) the Mosaic covenant is a covenant of works.

107. Gentry, *Kingdom through Covenant*, 63–64

108. Swain, *Trinity, Revelation, and Reading*, 25. Swain correctly notes that the loci of progressive unity is not found in cultural, historical, or literary features of revelation—these features evince immense diversity. The source of unity is christocentric; it lies with the Word, that is, God's Word spoken by the prophets, then apostles.

109. Evans, "Inaugurating the Kingdom," 50.

110. Ladd, *Presence of the Future*, 331.

> . . . the kingdom of God is the redemptive reign of God dynamically active to establish his rule among men, and that this kingdom, which will appear as an apocalyptic act at the end of the age, has already come into human history in the person and mission of Jesus to overcome evil, to deliver men from its power, and to bring them into the blessings of God's reign. The kingdom of God involves two great moments: fulfillment within history and consummation at the end of history.[111]

In Second Temple rabbinic theology, regarding the kingdom of God, God's reign was present, but present through the law. This meant that the catalyst rested with man either accepting or rejecting God's reign and rule by means of obedience to the law. The only coming of the kingdom that could be conceived by the rabbis was the "eschatological manifestation at the end of the age."[112] However, the kingdom of God that Jesus preached was *sui generis*. That is to say, in the person and work of Jesus, God takes the initiative. In Jesus, God is manifesting his reign in Christ as God's vicegerent. The signs of the kingdom—for example, casting out demons, the fall of Satan, miracles, preaching of the gospel, forgiveness of sins[113]—all point to the present kingdom of God, not the imminent, apocalyptic approaching of God's reign. In Jesus' coming, God has already entered into history as the Messiah-King[114] to achieve redemption; in principle, the kingdom is realized in this present age, and will be fully realized in the age to come.[115] This is the nature of the kingdom of God: it's *"theopolitical"* in that it is the "saving rule of God.[116] And it demands our use (in spite of its misuse and abuse), because in Christ God's reign is manifested in this age and the age to come! In short, the kingdom of God is the *Missio Dei*[117] through Jesus Christ as God's vicegerent, also known as mediatorial king. Both the

---

111. Ladd, *Presence of the Future*, 218.
112. Ladd, *Presence of the Future*, 238.
113. Hoekema, *Bible and the Future*, 46–47.
114. Gamble, *Whole Counsel of God*, 508.
115. Vos, *Pauline Eschatology*, 37–38.
116. Clowney, "Politics of the Kingdom," 293.

117. Bosch, *Transforming Mission*, 389. Bosch defines the Missio Dei as: "God's self-revelation as the One who loves the world, God's involvement in and with the world, the nature and activity of God, which embraces both the church and the world, and in which the church is privileged to participate. Missio Dei enunciates the good news that God is a God-for-people." Bosch correctly notes that the mission of God is first not the activity of the church in the world, but first the activity of God in the world as the church participates with God. The primary agent is God not the church.

inauguration (kingdom dominion) and consummation (kingdom domain) of the kingdom of God is a work of God and God alone.

CHAPTER 2

Inaugurated Eschatology and the Two-Ages Model

Now that we have a biblically based and theologically coherent definition for the kingdom of God motif, let us focus on a particular schema of eschatology regarding God's present victorious reign in Christ Jesus[1] through his church in history, that is in this present age, namely inaugurated eschatology.[2] In other words, how are we to understand God's victorious reign within history, and God's victorious reign within history through his church as a theological foundation that can also serve as a model of orientation for helping Christians (individually and corporately) navigate the missional landscape. In short, just as with one's broad notion of the kingdom of God, likewise one's eschatological approach will affect one's understanding of the nature and practice of missions. Mission creep is a real concern for the contemporary church, and how one understands both the definition of the kingdom of God, in general, and eschatology, in particular, affects said understanding and engagement.

How do we understand God's reign in real time, God's victorious reign in Christ Jesus and his church in history in this age, in spite of cultural declension and dissonance, that is, the historical, cultural, and societal conflict and conceptual dialectic between this present age—an age

---

1. Gaffin, "Theonomy and Eschatology."

2. Gaffin, "Theonomy and Eschatology," 216. Gaffin notes that the formal structure of eschatology is an eschatology of victory: "Most assuredly, the eschatology of the New Testament is an 'eschatology of victory'—victory presently being realized by and for the church, through the eschatological kingship of the exalted Christ (Eph. 1:22)."

Inaugurated Eschatology and the Two-Ages Model

of corruption and rebellion—and God's reign? David Wells describes the radicality and universality of our cultural dissonance:

> What is striking about our culture today is that its corruption is not simply at the edges. It is not simply found among the cultured elite . . . It is not simply found among postmodern academics... or among vicious street gangs, or among rappers who spew forth obscenities and violence, or among the venders of pornography, or in the bizarre and unashamed revelations of deeply private matters that are aired on television talk shows. What is striking is that this corruption is ubiquitous. It is not located in this or that pocket of depravity, but is spread like a dense fog throughout our society. It is even spread by those who are safe, ordinary, dull, and dimwitted, not merely by the incendiary and bellicose, the subversive and anti-social.[3]

So again, in light of our present moment of cultural dissonance, how can we speak of the victorious reign of Christ and his church in this present age, which includes this present moment of cultural dissension, a moment (by the way) which is exponentially worse today in 2021 than it was when Wells penned these words?[4] As Gary North contends, there has to be more to God's reign in Christ through his church in this age in spite of the seeming cultural declension and defeat in history.[5] Before we take a look at the present or inaugurated reign of God in Christ by means of the resurrection, and that reign of God in Christ in relation to Christ's church as the eschatological end-time temple, let us first take a look at what is meant by this present age in history, and then, secondly, inaugurated eschatology.

THE TWO-AGES MODEL

How do we frame history? What are some of the models at our disposal? Broadly speaking, there are three views of history: ancient, atheistic, and Christian.[6] The first is the Greek view of history. This view must be rejected because it is cyclical in nature: that is, history is nothing more or nothing less than a repeated cycle. There may be individual goals in life, but no

---

3. Wells, "Our Dying Culture," 25–26.
4. I am thinking specifically of the moral insanity of same-sex marriage and the transgender revolution.
5. North, *Westminster's Confession*, 184.
6. Hoekema, *Bible and the Future*, 24–33.

goal of history.[7] If time is cyclical, then history is meaningless, making "the events of history devoid of significance."[8] This affects the notion of redemption. Time, for the Greek, was something to be delivered from, delivered from the enslavement of time's "eternal circular course in which everything keeps recurring."[9] This makes the biblical notions of the kingdom of God, redemptive history, and eschatology unthinkable to the ancient Greeks. And conversely, the Greek view of history must be rejected for it does not see that God has a purpose for history, that history is moving inexorably toward God's goal of consummate reign, when all enemies will be his footstool.[10]

The second interpretative model of time and history to be rejected is the atheistic, existential view.[11] History is a meaningless meandering toward nothingness; history is a succession of random events. On the macro level, life is meaningless. Yet, on the micro level of individual human existence, life can be meaningful when each individual makes meaning by making significant decisions that are subjectively significant. Yet, there is no objective sense of meaning, much less a metanarrative, eschatological meaning.

In contrast to these views, there is the Christian interpretation of history. What is the Christian view of time and history? William Green says,

> The Bible is largely a book of history. But it is a special kind of history, the history of God's dealings with man. Man was created by God, then sinned against him and was punished by death. God provided a plan for his restoration, calling the faithful out of the world of sinners to become his servants, his chosen people. With Abraham he made a covenant, promising that in him and in his seed should all the nations of the earth be blessed. That covenant was renewed when God called Israel out of Egypt under Moses, and gave them his law, with promises and warnings for the obedient and the disobedient. All the subsequent history of Israel under judges, kings, and foreign oppressors is interpreted as the fulfillment of God's promises, his chastisement, and his mercy. God uses even the heathen as his tools, the "rod of his anger," to scourge his perverse people. Then upon the heathen too he executes judgment,

---

7. Hoekema, *Bible and the Future*, 24.

8. Hoekema, *Bible and the Future*, 24. Quote from Marsh, *Fullness of Time*, 167.

9. Hoekema, *Bible and the Future*, 24. Quote from Cullman, *Christ and Time*, 52.

10. For an insightful early apostolic use of Psalm 110:1 in developing a New Testament inaugurated eschatology, see Stewart, "Temporary Messianic Kingdom."

11. Hoekema, *Bible and The Future*, 25.

INAUGURATED ESCHATOLOGY AND THE TWO-AGES MODEL

> for he is the god of all the earth, and none can escape his wrath. Through his prophets he speaks, calling his people to repentance, promising them a Prince, his anointed one, who would usher in a new covenant and a new kingdom better than the old. The New Testament is the declaration that all the purposes and promises of God are fulfilled in Jesus of Nazareth, born as a man from David's line, but at the same time the only begotten Son of God. He is the King of God's people, but his kingdom is not of this world. Those whom God now calls he translates out of the kingdom of darkness into the kingdom of the Son of his love. As partakers of his Spirit, they now enjoy the blessings of love, joy, and peace, even while they suffer great tribulation, but their hope goes beyond this life to the time of the resurrection, when they shall be clothed with a new spiritual body, like that of their risen Lord.[12]

In short, the Christian interpretation of history and time is the kingdom of God. God's reign interprets all of history; that is to say, sacred history interprets secular history. Hoekema posits five hermeneutical features of said Christian interpretation of history and time: history is a working out of God's purposes; God is the Lord of history; Christ is the center of history; the new age has already been ushered in; and all of history is moving toward a goal. These are the five hermeneutical features of a Christian interpretation of history and time.[13] Out of these five features, let us look at the fourth: that is, the new age has already been ushered in.

What does Hoekema mean by "new age"? By definition, the new is in contradistinction to the old. Ridderbos sees in this two-ages model of history the warp and woof of Pauline preaching:

> Before everything else, he [Paul] was the proclaimer of a new time . . . the intrusion of a new world aeon. Such was the dominating perspective and foundation of Paul's entire preaching. . . . The person of Jesus Christ forms the mystery and middle point of this great historical redemptive revelation. Because Christ is revealed, a new aeon has been ushered in, the old world has ended, and the new world has begun.[14]

If the two-ages model is true, then it has at least two eschatological implications: first, it explains how in part the new age has already been ushered in, that the kingdom of God is inaugurated; second, it has implications for

---

12. Green "Christian View of History," 99–100.
13. Hoekema, *Bible and the Future*, 25–32.
14. Ridderbos, *Paul and Jesus*, 155–56.

the proponents of premillennialism (post-Parousia) and postmillennialism (pre-Parousia).

Biblical Evidence of the Two-Ages Model

Before we address the two implications, let's address the biblical feasibility of the two-ages model.[15] Does the New Testament teach a two-ages model of history? What is meant by "age"? "Age," in both Hebrew and Greek,[16] is an indefinite elongated period of time. It can refer to a backward or forward look to time or both.[17] Bruce says,

> The distinction between the present age and the age to come is commonly made in the NT, but with a peculiarly Christian modification. The present age is evil (Gal. 1:4); in the age to come, which follows the resurrection and judgment, righteousness will reign (cf. 2 Pet. 3:13). . . . While "eternal life" (*zōē aiōnios*) etymologically might mean simply life of indefinite or perpetual duration, it appears from its NT usage to mean more precisely "the life of the age to come," i.e., resurrection life. . . . Here is the distinctive feature in NT teaching about the two ages. The age to come is the age of the kingdom of God.[18]

Also, Sasse notes that "age" is constitutive of both the idea of prolonged, limited time and unending time. He says, "The concept of limited and unlimited time merge in the word αἰών. This implied inner contradiction is brought to light in the expression χρόνος αἰώνιος which is used as an equivalent of the plur. in Romans 16:25; 2 Timothy 1:9; Titus 1:2; for eternal time is strictly a contradiction in terms."[19] More will be said about the kingdom of God as both the eternal age to come and this present age—that is, the age of unlimited time and the present age of prolonged limited time—but

---

15. When the distinction is made between two-ages— this age and the age to come— this is not to say that there are no dispensations subsumed within this present age vis-à-vis the age to come. In this sense one can say there are ages or dispensations within this present age: for example, the antediluvian age, the postdiluvian age, the patriarchal age, the Mosaic age, the Davidic age, etc. Dr. C. J. Williams helpfully reminded me of the "former days" of the Old Testament in contradiction to the "latter days" that began with the inauguration of the kingdom of God in Christ and the apostolic church.

16. Bruce, "Age," 67. See also Sasse, "αἰών," 198.

17. Bruce, "Age," 67.

18. Bruce, "Age," 68.

19. Sasse, "αἰών," 199.

Inaugurated Eschatology and the Two-Ages Model

first, is Bruce correct? Is the distinction between this present age and the age to come a common motif with a particularly Christian modification of Second Temple Judaism? Second Temple Judaism posited not a two-ages model of time, but a three-ages model.[20] By 100 BC Jewish eschatology included a temporary political kingdom on earth as explained above, between this age and the eternal age to come of redemptive history; that is, the present age, an intermediate kingdom age, and the eternal age to come.[21] This distinction between the two ages is the eschatological warp and woof of the worldview of Second Temple Judaism.[22] Bailey says,

> The distinction between "this age" and "the age to come" is a basic one in the thinking of Judaism. The point need not be labored that the prophetic hope of the Old Testament period contemplated a golden age for Israel which should bring the history of the nation to consummation in a new historical and national era. Nor is it necessary to give the evidence for the development in Judaism of a transcendental hope according to which there would be established a new heaven and a new earth ushered in by a universal judgment and introducing the eternal reign of God. This conception involved the cessation of the present order and the establishment of a new one. But the old national hope persisted, and it became necessary for those who held the two conceptions to harmonize them. By the logic of the case, if the Messianic future of the nation was to be followed by a heavenly kingdom of eternal duration, then the Messianic era could be only a temporary one.[23]

This explains why our Lord's contemporaries and his disciples expected an intermediate political kingdom age between this present age and the age to come. Suffice it to say, Jesus modified this three-ages schema by rejecting the political, messianic era in affirmation of a two-ages schema.[24] Do Jesus and the biblical writers affirm a two-ages model of redemptive history? Is the concept of the two-ages model well established by the New Testament?

20. Waymeyer, *Amillennialism and the Age to Come*, 94.
21. Charles, *Eschatology*, 167–361.
22. Bailey, "Temporary Messianic Reign," 170.
23. Bailey, "Temporary Messianic Reign," 170–71.
24. Though premillennialism (especially the dispensational variety) posits that the political Messianic Age is not rejected, but delayed, I am arguing that if the concept of the two ages is well established in the New Testament and assumed by Jesus and the biblical writers, then such a schema precludes a three-ages model of redemptive history, whether it's the Messianic Age of Second Temple Judaism, premillennialism, or dispensational premillennialism, etc.

The phraseology of "this age" and/or "the age to come" is well attested in the New Testament; Matthew 12:32: "And whoever speaks a word against the Son of Man will be forgiven, but whoever speaks against the Holy Spirit will not be forgiven, either in this age or in the age to come." Notice that the phraseology of "this age or in the age to come" encompass all of time, that is, limited time and unending or eternal time. The unpardonable sin is an eternal sin. In other words, Jesus describes an eternally unforgiven sin and eternal judgment by employing two-ages phraseology.

Matthew 13:40: "Just as the weeds are gathered and burned with fire, so will it be at the end of the age." The end of the age is the last day of this present age, that is, the day of judgment. The line of demarcation in context is the return of Christ in his second advent.

Matthew 24:3: "As he sat on the Mount of Olives, the disciples came to him privately, saying, 'Tell us, when will these things be, and what will be the sign of your coming and of the end of the age?'" A characteristic of this age is temporality, that is, this age is coming to an end.

Matthew 28:20: "teaching them to observe all that I have commanded you. And behold, I am with you always, to the end of the age." The Great Commission will continue in this age and Christ has promised to be with his church to the end of this age; that is, the gospel age terminates when this present age ends.

Mark 10:30: "who will not receive a hundredfold now in this time, houses and brothers and sisters and mothers and children and lands, with persecutions, and in the age to come eternal life." The operative phraseology used here is "this time" vis-à-vis "the age to come." The former "time" is a synonym for "age." This time or age is constitutive of temporal blessings (what we call common grace); such blessings are, for example, shelter, property, familial relations, etc.—along with temporal hardship such as persecution.

Luke 16:8: "The master commended the dishonest manager for his shrewdness. For the sons of this world are more shrewd in dealing with their own generation than the sons of light." The phrase "sons of this age" is in contradistinction to "sons of light." The implications are that the age to come is the age of light vis-à-vis the age of this present darkness; and that the sons of this age are children of darkness and the sons of the age to come are children of light.

Luke 18:30: "who will not receive many times more in this time, and in the age to come eternal life." As noted, "this time" is a synonym for "this age."

Luke 20:34–36: "And Jesus said to them, 'The sons of this age marry and are given in marriage, but those who are considered worthy to attain to that age and to the resurrection from the dead neither marry nor are given in marriage, for they cannot die anymore, because they are equal to angels and are sons of God, being sons of the resurrection.'" More will be said about this passage, but suffice it to say these two ages are not only quantitatively different—that is, limited time vis-à-vis unlimited or eternal time—but also qualitatively different, that is, a natural order/world vis-à-vis a supernatural order/world (new heavens and earth).[25]

Romans 12:2: "And do not be conformed to this world, but be transformed by the renewing of your mind, that you may prove what is that good and acceptable and perfect will of God." The term translated here as "world" is "age." Paul contrasts this age and the age to come in ethical terms (axiology) in contradistinction to quantitative (duration) and qualitative (order) terms.

First Corinthians 1:20: "Where is the one who is wise? Where is the scribe? Where is the debater of this age? Has not God made foolish the wisdom of the world?" The philosopher of this age is formed and informed by the wisdom of this age. By contrast, the wisdom of this age is foolishness compared to the wisdom of the age to come, a wisdom from above instantiated at the cross.

First Corinthians 2:6, 8: "Yet among the mature we do impart wisdom, although it is not a wisdom of this age or of the rulers of this age, who are doomed to pass away. . . . None of the rulers of this age understood this, for if they had, they would not have crucified the Lord of glory." Three times the phrase "this age" is described both as the world's wisdom and the world's rulers, in contrast to the wisdom of God implied in the age to come. Both the wisdom of this age and rulers of this age are devoid of divine wisdom.

Second Corinthians 4:4: "In their case the god of this world has blinded the minds of the unbelievers, to keep them from seeing the light of the gospel of the glory of Christ, who is the image of God." This age is described as darkness in contrast with the light of the age to come. Satan is the god of this dark age; Christ is Lord concerning the gospel light of glory.

---

25. Though these two orders/ages are qualitatively different, there is nonetheless continuity and discontinuity. See Busenitz, "Kingdom of God."

Galatians 1:4: "who gave himself for our sins to deliver us from the present evil age, according to the will of our God and Father." Christ's death on the cross delivers us from our sins and "the present evil age."

Ephesians 1:21: "far above all rule and authority and power and dominion, and above every name that is named, not only in this age but also in the one to come." As God's vicegerent, Christ reigns now in this age and forever in the age to come. The age to come points to the exalted rank of Christ being eternal, not temporal; Christ's kingdom is not limited to this present age but is eternal in the age to come.

Ephesians 2:2: "in which you once walked according to the course of this world, according to the prince of the power of the air, the spirit who now works in the sons of disobedience." The phrase "walked according to the course of this world" is a graphic portrayal of a life dominated by Satan in this age, that is, "the prince of the power of the air" over "the sons of disobedience"; that is, children of Satan.

First Timothy 6:17–19: "As for the rich in this present age, charge them not to be haughty, nor to set their hopes on the uncertainty of riches, but on God, who richly provides us with everything to enjoy. They are to do good, to be rich in good works, to be generous and ready to share, thus storing up treasure for themselves as a good foundation for the future, so that they may take hold of that which is truly life." The contrast is not only storing up treasure in this present age vis-à-vis storing up treasure for the future, that is, the age to come, but also between this present life and the life to come, that is, "truly life."

Titus 2:12: "training us to renounce ungodliness and worldly passions, and to live self-controlled, upright, and godly lives in the present age." The Christian life in this present age is to be lived in light of the age to come, the age to come implied in verse 13 regarding the blessed hope of Christ's second coming, which marks the end of the old age (present age) and the beginning of the new age (the age to come).

Hebrews 6:5: "and have tasted the goodness of the word of God and the powers of the age to come." The powers of the age to come are supernatural, that is, the miraculous gifts of the Holy Spirit during the apostolic period. These miracles were the intrusion of the future supernatural order into the natural order.

From the biblical data, Jesus and Paul and the author of Hebrews spoke of two successive, qualitatively and quantitatively distinct periods: the former protological and the latter eschatological. Vos correctly argues

Inaugurated Eschatology and the Two-Ages Model

that these two ages are a "direct successiveness."[26] This presents a problem for the premillennialist[27] who posits an intermediate age. Based on the biblical evidence, there is no intermediate age. The consensus of Second Temple Judaism was that the intermediate age was of limited duration, that at the latter end of the first century "there was also a very definite proposal on the part of certain teachers to place the limit at 1,000 years."[28] There is no evidence of this teaching in the New Testament. It's clear from both Christ Jesus and Paul that there are only two ages that are successive. As Vos says,

> The starting point is the historico-dramatic conception of the two successive ages. These two ages are distinguished as . . . "this age," "the present age" [and] "that age," "the future age" . . . from the way in which it occurs in the teaching of Jesus and Paul it appears to have been current at the time.[29]

Based on the biblical data, this age and the age to come can be characterized in five ways. First, this age and the age to come are both exhaustive of all time, including eternity, that is, endless time in Matthew 12:32 and Mark 3:29. In Mark it speaks of "an eternal sin." It's clear that these two ages are exhaustive. This is also suggested by Mark 10:29–30, where the "age to come" is itself eternal life. Also, Matthew 12:32 and Mark 10:32 both imply that this present age originated at the beginning of human history as recorded in Genesis 1–3 because this age is not of recent origin; that is to say, it's not inaugurated with Christ's first advent, but already present at the very beginning of Jesus' ministry. The phrase "the sons of this age marry" (Luke 20:34) implies what's constitutive of the protological order of creation. Phrases like "present evil age" (Gal 1:4) and "god of this age" (2 Cor 4:4), imply the fall of creation. In short, this age and the age to come originated at the beginning of human history into all eternity. By necessary deduction, there is no period of history before this present age, and no period of history between this present age and the age to come, which precludes chiliasm.

Second, this age and the age to come are qualitatively different periods in world history and states of human existence. Both Luke 20:34–36 and

---

26. Vos, *Pauline Eschatology*, 25.

27. For a summary view of the nature of the millennial debate, see Bock, ed., *Three Views on the Millennium*; Clouse, ed., *Meaning of the Millennium*; Erickson, *Contemporary Options in Eschatology*; Cohn, *Pursuit of the Millennium*.

28. Bailey, "Temporary Messianic Reign," 187.

29. Vos, "Eschatology of the New Testament," 28.

Matthew 13:24–30, 36–43 evince respectively a natural and supernatural order, both qualitatively distinct. This age does not evolve through a natural or gradual process into the age to come. According to Luke 20:27–40, in this age we have marriage, death and dying, and natural men, where both the righteous and the wicked are synchronous. In contradistinction to this age, in the age to come there is no marriage, no death and no dying, resurrected men, and only the worthy as the sons of God attaining the eternal age. According to Matthew 13:24–30, 36–43, in this present age we have wheat (sons of the kingdom) mixed with tares (sons of the evil one) in a natural state or condition. In contradistinction, in the age to come there is only the wheat (sons of the kingdom) in a glorified state or condition.

Third, this age is and will always be evil. In other words, this age's basic characteristic is morally evil. Case in point: Luke 16:8 depicts the "sons of this age" as evil in contrast to the sons of light in the age to come. Mark 10:30 teaches that in this age we must expect persecution for the gospel's sake. In Romans 12:2, Paul's exhorts Christians not to be conformed to this age, meaning do not conform to the evil template of this age. Second Corinthians 4:4 notes that Satan is the "god of this age," making this age evil. Galatians 1:4 recognizes that this age is a "present, evil age." Ephesians 2:2 describes the former wicked lives of the Ephesians as "walking according to the course of this world." The implication is that the wickedness of this age is inveterate; that is, this age will always be characterized as an age of evil, as an age of persecuted Christians, and an age where Satan will always be its god. If this is the case, then there is never coming a day when Christians will not be persecuted, never coming a day when conforming to this age for the Christian will never be a temptation.

Fourth, we currently are in the last days of this age. Paul stresses the fact that this age is nearing the end: "Yet among the mature we do impart wisdom, although it is not a wisdom of this age or of the rulers of this age, who are doomed to pass away" (1 Cor 2:6). John stresses the same reality: "And the world is passing away, and the lust of it; but he who does the will of God abides forever" (1 John 2:17). We see the same thing when the author of Hebrews says, "He then would have had to suffer often since the foundation of the world; but now, once at the end of the ages, He has appeared to put away sin by the sacrifice of Himself" (Heb 9:26). Likewise, Paul says, "Now all these things happened to them as examples, and they were written for our admonition, upon whom the ends of the ages have come" (1 Cor

Inaugurated Eschatology and the Two-Ages Model

10:11). In short, since the first coming of Christ and his resurrection, this age has been nearing its end, that is, the last days of this present age.

Fifth, there is the "already" and "not yet" dialectic. The blessings of the age to come have "already," in part, broken into this age and are operative in this age, but have "not yet" been consummated. This is what is meant by "inaugurated eschatology," that is to say, the victory of God's reign in Christ is realized in principle though not in consummated realization.

The Implications of the Two-Ages Model

As stated above, the two-ages model as an interpreted grid poses some problems to both premillennialism and postmillennialism. Regarding the former, Scripture explicitly teaches that there is a stark line of demarcation that separates this age and the age to come: that is, Christ's Second Advent. Christ's Second Advent is constitutive of eschatological judgment. Our Lord is very clear when he says in Matthew 13:39–40, 49–50,

> The enemy who sowed them is the devil, the harvest is the end of the age, and the reapers are the angels. Therefore, as the tares are gathered and burned in the fire, so it will be at the end of this age. . . . So, it will be at the end of the age. The angels will come forth, separate the wicked from among the just, and cast them into the furnace of fire. There will be wailing and gnashing of teeth.

In contrast, the premillenarians contend that said judgment will not occur at our Lord's return, but a thousand years later after the millennial reign.[30] Yet, Scripture is clear that at our Lord's return judgment will immediately occur: "When the Son of Man comes in his glory, and all the angels with him, then he will sit on his glorious throne. Before him will be gathered all the nations, and he will separate people one from another as a shepherd separates the sheep from the goats" (Matt 25:31–32). Not only does judgment occur at our Lord's return, but so does cosmic regeneration (2 Pet 3:3–15) and the resurrection (1 Cor 15:35–57). As Riddlebarger rightly contends, "Scripture clearly teaches that the resurrection and the judgement of the righteous and the unrighteous will occur at the same time, thus eliminating the possibility of an earthly millennial age to dawn after the Lord's return."[31]

---

30. Walvoord, *Millennial Kingdom*, 128–33.
31. Riddlebarger, *Case for Amillennialism*, 166.

Even though the two-ages model precludes the possibility of an earthly, post-Parousia premillennial age, the pre-Parousia notions of both amillennialism and postmillennialism are consistent with the two-ages model. Both pre-Parousian schemas are one species of doctrine, essentially agree in the overall structure of the eschatological framework of the New Testament: that is, this age and the age to come. There will be a general resurrection (not multiple), judgment (not judgments separated by a thousand years), and cosmic regeneration—all happening after our Lord's return. Both notions of pre-Parousianism have this in common.[32] Where postmillenarians and amillenarians disagree is over the notion of victory regarding the nature of the kingdom of God, later to be addressed. However, there are some problems that the two-ages model poses for postmillennialism. Riddlebarger posits two critical questions to postmillennialists. First, will there be a gradual amelioration of evil in this present evil age? Second, will Jesus return to a saved world as according to Warfield?[33] Riddlebarger convincingly argues that based on a two-ages model, ". . . we can answer both of the preceding questions in the negative. . . . The secular, economic, cultural, and political factors" of this age will not be transformed by the amelioration of evil because this present age will continue to be defined as being evil and (I will add) under the sway of the Satan, who is the god of this age.[34] In short, the nature of this present age, in light of the two-ages model, precludes the dissolution of said cultural dissonance in this present age. With the ebb and flow of history, cultural and political triumphs and declensions are inherent cycles and patterns of this age.

INAUGURATED ESCHATOLOGY

Back to the question of inaugurated eschatology, what is inaugurated eschatology? Beale defines inaugurated eschatology as the following:

> . . . in the NT the end of days predicted by the OT are seen as beginning fulfillment with Christ's first coming and will culminate in a final consummated fulfillment as the very end of history. All

---

32. Another aspect of general continuity between amillennialism and postmillennialism is the generic notion of inaugurated eschatology, i.e., the great eschatological realities of the age to come have already broken into this present age by means of the kingdom of God.

33. Riddlebarger, *Case for Amillennialism*, 110.

34. Riddlebarger, *Case for Amillennialism*, 110.

that the OT foresaw would occur in the end times has begun already in the first century and continues on until the final coming of Christ.[35]

In short, inaugurated eschatology sees the consummated blessings of the kingdom age to come as having partially broken, in principle, into this present age. The future is made present. The future has been launched back into the present. The core expectations in the Old Testament are: the great tribulation, God's domination of gentiles, deliverance of Israel from oppressors, Israel's resurrection, the new covenant, the promised Spirit, the new creation, the new temple, the messianic king, and the establishment of God's kingdom—these expectations ". . . have been set in motion [sic] irreversibly by Christ's death and resurrection and the formation of the Christian church."[36] Beale notes that though some expectations were realized within the Old Testament period (for example, Israel's end-time restoration beginning at the time of the return of a faithful remnant from Babylon), said expectations were not "true" inaugurated expectations realized because they were not "irreversible conditions" because said conditions were frustrated by sin.[37]

In light of this definition, inaugurated eschatology is the means between the two extremes of an overrealized eschatology and underrealized eschatology.[38] An overrealized eschatology posits that the Christian has, more or less, the blessings from the future, in the age to come, realized now.[39] An underrealized eschatology fails to appreciate what the Christian possesses now in Christ.[40] An example of the former is sarcastically rejected by Paul:

> Already you have all you want! Already you have become rich! Without us you have become kings! And would that you did reign, so that we might share the rule with you! For I think that God has exhibited us apostles as last of all, like men sentenced to death, because we have become a spectacle to the world, to angels, and to men. We are fools for Christ's sake, but you are wise in Christ.

---

35. Beale, *New Testament Biblical Theology*, 162. See also Longenecker, *Paul, Apostle of Liberty*, 143.
36. Beale, *New Testament Biblical Theology*, 161.
37. Riddlebarger, *Case for Amillennialism*, 110.
38. Carson, "Partakers of the Age to Come," 91.
39. Carson, "Partakers of the Age to Come," 91.
40. Carson, "Partakers of the Age to Come," 92.

> We are weak, but you are strong. You are held in honor, but we in disrepute. To the present hour we hunger and thirst, we are poorly dressed and buffeted and homeless. (1 Cor 4:8–11).

An underrealized eschatology doesn't appreciate the power of God to change the believer. As Carson says, "You not only have the forgiveness of sin and the joy of being once and for all declared just before God . . . but also have ongoing cleansing from sin . . . to love what you didn't love and hate what you didn't hate." [41] An underrealized eschatology is framed by an "already" of this age while minimizing the "not yet" tension of the age to come. Conversely, an overrealized eschatology is framed by the "not yet" of the age to come while minimizing the "already" of this present age. Neither do justice to the inherent tension of the two-ages model. As Brower and Elliot contend,

> Both versions of the gospel are deficient. Without the firm hope for the future, symbolized by and inaugurated in the resurrection of Christ, the church's message proves to be fraudulent. And without the reality of God's action in Christ and its impact on this present age, the church seems to be a complete irrelevancy, only interested in conversations with itself. Its message to the world is drowned in the despair of human existence without God.[42]

In short, an inaugurated eschatology does justice to both the "already" partially realized eschatology of the age to come, as it overlaps this present age, and the "not yet" consummation of the eschatological age to come. The inherent dialectic is resolved in such an eschatological schema, making sense of our present cultural dissonance.

In summary, as noted above, based on the biblical data, this age and the age to come can be characterized in five ways. The first four ways have been summarily delineated: the two-ages model encompasses all of time; the two-ages model qualitatively delineates temporality from eternity; the two-ages model delineates this age as evil, and the age to come as holy without the presence of evil; and currently we are in the last days of this present age.

Next, there is the fifth characterization: the blessings of the age to come have "already," in part, broken into this age and are operative in this age, but have "not yet" been consummated. This, again as notes above, is

---

41. Carson, "Partakers of the Age to Come," 92.
42. Brower and Elliot, *Eschatology in the Bible*, v.

Inaugurated Eschatology and the Two-Ages Model

what is meant by inaugurated eschatology; that is to say, the victory of God's reign in Christ is realized in principle though not in consummated realization. The cultural dissonance of this present age is a present reality that will only be resolved at the end of this age. Inaugurated eschatology is the only eschatological schema that can make sense of the tension felt from our present cultural dissonance.

Inaugurated eschatology was also the schema that helped the apostles make sense of their cultural dissonance as well. Inaugurated eschatology was the mindset of the apostles, "a mindset for understanding the present within the climaxing context of redemptive history."[43] William Manson rightly contends that at the heart of inaugurated eschatology are two foci:

> When we turn to the New Testament, we pass from the climate of prediction to that of fulfillment. The things which God had foreshadowed by the lips of His holy prophets He has now, in part at least, brought to accomplishment. . . . The supreme sign of the Eschaton is the Resurrection of Jesus and the descent of the Holy Spirit on the Church. The Resurrection of Jesus is not simply a sign which God has granted in favour of His son, but is the [sic] inauguration, the entrance into history, of the times of the End.
>
> Christians, therefore, have entered through the Christ into the new age. . . . What has been predicted in the Holy Scriptures as to happen to Israel or to man in the Eschaton has happened to and in Jesus. The foundation-stone of the New Creation has come into position.[44]

The Sign of the Eschaton: The Resurrection

Regarding the first foci, one of the clearest passages in the New Testament of the sign of the Eschaton as Christ's resurrection is in Hebrews 6:4–6:

> For it is impossible, in the case of those who have once been enlightened, who have tasted the heavenly gift, and have shared in the Holy Spirit, and have tasted the goodness of the word of God and the powers of the age to come, and then have fallen away, to restore them again to repentance, since they are crucifying once again the Son of God to their own harm and holding him up to contempt. (Heb 6:4–6)

43. Gladd and Harmon, *Making All Things New*, 4.
44. Quoted in Beale, "Eschatological Conception," 17.

"[T]he powers of the age to come" is a reference to miracles, that is to say, the miraculous sign gifts that accompanied the message of the kingdom at the inauguration of the kingdom age, that is, the gospel age. Those sign gifts announced the inauguration of the age to come. The age to come is equivalent to the reign of Christ. According to both Hebrews 2:9 and Ephesians 2:9, the reign of Christ has already begun; conversely, this means that the age to come has already begun.

The performance of miracles is one of the signs of the presence or inauguration of the eschatological kingdom of the age to come, that is, the miracles performed by Jesus and his disciples. In Matthew 11:4–6, in response to John the Baptist, Jesus indicates that the kingdom has been inaugurated, an inauguration made evident by miracles. Jesus says: "Go and tell John the things which you hear and see: The blind see and the lame walk; the lepers are cleansed and the deaf hear; the dead are raised up and the poor have the gospel preached to them." Yet, these miracles were only signs of the kingdom. They had limitations due to the kingdom coming in part, not in consummation. Evidence of the provisional nature of these miracles corresponding to the present, partial nature of the kingdom was the fact that not all of the sick were healed; not all the dead were raised; not all the lame were made to walk; and eventually death took those who were healed and raised. The premier, miraculous sign of the Eschaton is the irreversible resurrection of Christ. The age to come is the age of the resurrection according to Luke:

> And Jesus said to them, "The sons of this age marry and are given in marriage, but those who are considered worthy to attain to that age and to the resurrection from the dead neither marry nor are given in marriage, for they cannot die anymore, because they are equal to angels and are sons of God, being sons of the resurrection. (Luke 20:34–36)

The age to come is the supernatural age of the resurrection. Christ's resurrection as the sign of the Eschaton is the supernatural age to come; it is also the age of new creation; it is also the kingdom of God breaking into this present age—all three are facets of the Eschaton.

The Resurrection and New Creation

What is the relation between the kingdom of God, Christ's resurrection, and new creation? G. K. Beale is most helpful at this point. Beale builds on

Inaugurated Eschatology and the Two-Ages Model

the notion that the "already and not yet" schema of inaugurated eschatology is crucial in understanding the New Testament as a heuristic lens. He states that his ". . . thesis goes beyond this perspective by attempting to define the general notion of eschatology specifically as new creation."[45] If eschatology, in general, and inaugurated eschatology, in particular, forms and informs all of New Testament biblical theology, as Vos taught, then should not inaugurated eschatology ". . . shed light on all the other major theological doctrines of the New Testament?"

But how does inaugurated eschatology shed light on all the major doctrines? Beale proposes a center for a comprehensive biblical theology. A number of biblical theologians favor a multiperspectival approach over a single approach. Case in point is C. H. H. Scobie. He says:

> The attempt in the late 18th and early 19th centuries to develop a purely historical and descriptive independent Biblical Theology soon split into separate Old Testament and New Testament Theologies which in turn were succeeded by studies of the religion of ancient Israel and the early Church. . . . It is difficult to understand the obsession with finding one single theme or "centre" for Old Testament or New Testament Theology and still less for an entire Biblical Theology. It is widely held today that the quest for a single centre has failed. An approach which recognizes several themes would appear to be more productive and this seems to be the trend in a number of more recent Old Testament Theologies including those of J.L. McKenzie, W. Zimmerli, W.A. Dryness and C. Westermann.[46]

Beale rejects this multiperspectival approach in favor of a center, an overarching center that's more overarching than other proposed centers. Beale's center approach is a refinement of eschatology, in general, and inaugurated eschatology, in particular, as being a center of biblical theology. What is that refinement? He proposes "new creation." Beale contends that for this biblical theological approach to succeed it will have to show how a single theme of new creation can relate to two things: (1) how new creation relates to various major theological doctrines in the New Testament and (2) the New Testament books themselves. For the purpose of this project, I will relate the former to missions in the next chapter.

---

45. Beale, "Eschatological Conception," 11.
46. Scobie, "Structure of Biblical Theology," 163, 178–79.

Kingdom Theology

How does new creation relate to the resurrection, which William Manson contends is the foundation stone of new creation? Beale first begins with the biblical notion of end times. To have a full-orbed notion of biblical theology, in general, and New Testament biblical theology, in particular, one must have a biblical notion of the final phase of history or the end of the age—for example, the rapture, tribulation, the resurrection, the judgment, etc.—and how that relates to the events of the death and resurrection of Christ. The beginning of Christian history was perceived by the first Christians as the beginning of the end times. D. C. Allison recognizes that much of New Testament scholarship has been too atomistic. Christ's death and resurrection haven't been studied with a view to their eschatological implications; "Christian theology has rarely grappled seriously with the eschatological presuppositions that permeate the New Testament."[47] Contrary to this, Christian theology must grapple with the fact that for first-century Christians the beginning of Christian history was perceived as the beginning of the end times.[48] A brief survey of the New Testament will evince that the phrase "latter days" occurs twenty-seven times in the New Testament, including synonyms.[49] Most of those end-times phrases are used to describe the end times as an "already" event that has happened in the first century.

Beale's first observation is that these New Testament end-times phraseologies are allusions to identical phrases in the Old Testament. The difference is that in the Old Testament the wording is proleptic, anticipating a future time. Beale says in this future time:

> (1) There will be a tribulation for Israel consisting of oppression (Ezekiel 38:14–17ff.), persecution (Daniel 10:14ff.; 11:27–12:10), false teaching, deception and apostasy (Daniel10:14ff.; 11:27–35); (2) after tribulation Israel will seek the Lord (Hosea 3:4–5), they will be delivered (Ezekiel 38:14–16ff., Daniel 10:14ff.; 12:1–13) and their enemies will be judged (Ezekiel 38:14–16ff.; Daniel 10:14ff.; 11:40–45; 12:2); (3) this deliverance and judgment will occur because a leader (Messiah) from Israel will finally conquer all of its gentile enemies (Genesis 49:1,8–12; Numbers 24:14–19; Isaiah 2:2–4; Micah 4:1–3; Daniel 2:28–45; 10:14–12:10; (4) God will establish a kingdom on the earth and rule over it (Isaiah 2:2–4; Micah 4:1–3; Daniel 2:28–45) together with a Davidic king (Hosea

---

47. Allison, *End of the Ages*, 169.
48. Beale, "Eschatological Conception," 12.
49. Beale, "Eschatological Conception," 13.

3:4–5); (5) after the time of tribulation and persecution, Daniel 11–12 says there will be a resurrection of the righteous and unrighteous (see Daniel 11:30—12:3ff.).[50]

The technical eschatological vocabulary of the Old Testament (as well as less formal terminology), is picked up and utilized in the New Testament. This technical eschatological vocabulary of the "latter days" and "end times," etc., has identical meaning in both the Old and New Testaments, with one exception: "In the New Testament the end-days predicted by the Old Testament are seen as beginning their fulfillment with Christ's first coming."[51] All that the Old Testament prophets predicted would come to pass in the "last days" have "already" been set in motion by the "life, death, resurrection and formation of the Christian church" by Christ's first coming. Beale observes that both the resurrection of Christ and Pentecost "signalled the inauguration of [Christ's] rule through the church," that is, the messianic reign.[52] In short, the latter days are occurring throughout the entirety of the messianic age throughout the church age. Christ is ruling and reigning through the church, including the twenty-first-century church. Beale notes that what the Old Testament prophets did not forecast or anticipate was that the kingdom of God and last-days tribulation would coexist, that they did not see what the apostle John saw, and that is that all three eschatological conditions—that is, tribulation, the kingdom, and perseverance—would coincide according to Revelation 1:9.[53]

Beale observes that when viewed from the perspective of the end times, New Testament doctrines are not radically altered, but "radically enriched."[54] The central event that inaugurated the last days was the resurrection of Christ, what Manson noted in the above quote as the foundational stone of new creation. In short, what has been ushered in is the "end-time new creation."[55] Beale convincingly argues that the resurrection by definition is the inauguration of end-times new creation. In fact, he says, "New creation is in mind wherever the concept of resurrection occurs, since it is essentially the new creation of humanity."[56] Understood in light

50. Beale, "Eschatological Conception," 14.
51. Beale, "Eschatological Conception," 14.
52. Beale, "Eschatological Conception," 15.
53. More will be said about this condition below.
54. Beale, "Eschatological Conception," 18.
55. Beale, "Eschatological Conception," 18.
56. Beale, "Eschatological Conception," 19.

Kingdom Theology

of eschatological new creation, the death of Christ is the "beginning of the destruction of the entire world, which will be consummated" at the end of the age.[57] New creation, as a biblical theological center, is instantiated in the resurrection so much so that the resurrection as the inaugurated sign of the Eschaton is equivalent to new creation. Beale argues that the reason why the resurrection is conceptually equivalent to new creation is because the mode by which redeemed humanity participates in new creation is through newly created, glorified, resurrected bodies.[58] This is apparent in a number of texts: 2 Corinthians 5:14–17; Colossians 1:15–18; Revelation 1:5 and 3:14. Resurrection is a new-creational event and construct. The actual terminology of "new creation" doesn't occur often in Paul; the actual phrase "new creation" occurs only twice, in 2 Corinthians 5:17 and Galatians 6:15. Yet paraphrastic variants, along with synonyms, are replete throughout the New Testament.[59] Resurrection is central in Paul,[60] and is the "climatic goal of the four Gospels, making the resurrection . . . a diamond which represents the new creation. [While] the various theological ideas are facets of the diamond . . ."[61]

The Kingdom of God and New Creation

In this cursory analysis, we can see the connection between last-days resurrection and new creation, with new creation being the eschatological center. Next, what is the relationship between the kingdom of God and new creation? Beale says that among some competitors against new creation vying for center, the notion of kingdom in the Gospels and Christ as Lord in the Pauline epistles (which is for Paul at core a kingdom of God motif) is a viable one. However, Beale convincingly argues that the kingdom of God is not a facet of new creation, nor is it more comprehensible of new creation, but "two sides of one coin."[62] How is this so? How is both the kingdom of God and new creation seen as "coequal?"[63] Beale says,

---

57. Beale, "Eschatological Conception," 19.
58. Beale, *New Testament Biblical Theology*, 227.
59. Beale, *New Testament Biblical Theology*, 23; see footnote 24.
60. See Gaffin, *Centrality of the Resurrection of Christ*; and Kim, *Origin of Paul*.
61. Beale, "Eschatological Conception," 23.
62. Beale, "Eschatological Conception," 25.
63. Beale, *New Testament Biblical Theology*, 171.

> Among some of the competing central ideas discussed, the most prominent competitors with that of the new-creational kingdom are the notions of "kingdom" by itself in the Gospels and of justification and reconciliation in the Pauline Epistles. The kingdom is a major facet of new creation, since Jesus was seen as reinstating the vice-regency that Adam should have successfully carried out of the original creation. But, just as in the first creation, the kingdom is so inextricably linked to new creation, that the two should be seen as co-equal. This is why I often refer to these two together as the "new-creational kingdom."[64]

Beale's argument is based on the original kingship or vicegerency of Adam. Beale says, "Kingship was to be a role of Adam in the original creation, and this is to be a feature of the consummated new creation according to Revelation 11:15 and 22:5."[65] The feature of the consummated new creation is the last Adam exercising his role of kingship over new creation. Christ as the last Adam reestablished the new creation as God's reigning vicegerent. God raised up Jesus Christ as the last Adamic figure to inaugurate a new creation, finding its consummation in the new heavens and earth.[66]

D. G. McCartney makes a similar argument. He contends that Jesus' establishment of the kingdom in the Gospels and throughout the New Testament is to be understood as "the reinstatement of the originally intended divine order for earth, with man properly situated as God's vicegerent."[67] McCartney points out that in the original kingship, Adam "spoiled his vicegerency." Because of this "earth was no longer compliant in its subjection to him."[68] McCartney argues that God created man in his image; in Genesis 5:3 "image" means man as son, and son means king, making man as image of God also mean son of God as king. In the original creation, God ruled the earth by means of the kingship of man's vicegerency.

Beale sees the connection between kingship and new creation in the context of Adam's commission in the first creation, and the subsequent passing on this commission to other Adamic figures, all typical of the last Adam, who is Christ.[69] Beale's storyline of the Old Testament goes as such:

---

64. Beale, *New Testament Biblical Theology*, 171.
65. Beale, "Eschatological Conception," 25.
66. Beale, "Eschatological Conception," 26.
67. McCartney, "Ecce Homo," 2.
68. McCartney, "Ecce Homo," 3.
69. Beale, *New Testament Biblical Theology*, 29–87.

> The Old Testament is the story of God, who progressively reestablishes his new-creational kingdom out of chaos over a sinful people by his word and Spirit through promise, covenant, and redemption, resulting in worldwide commission to the faithful to advance this kingdom and judgment (defeat or exile) for the unfaithful, unto his glory.[70]

Beale argues that the original commission in Genesis 1:26–28 involved the establishment of an eschatological kingdom of God where man (represented by Adam as federal head) would rule as God's vicegerent over new creation, that is, ". . . the yet to come escalated creation conditions to be a consummate 'eschatologically' enhanced stage of final blessedness."[71] The original Adamic Commission entailed a number of elements, summarized in Genesis 1:28 and reiterated and repeated for Abraham in the initial statement in Genesis 12:1–3 and to Israel; for example, Genesis 47:27; 48:3–4; Exodus 1:7; Numbers 23:10–11, just to name a few. The difference between the original Adamic Commission and the reinstatement after the fall is that the progeny is spiritual; that is, the progeny is expanded to include regenerate humanity, where a renewed regenerate humanity reigns over unregenerate humanity and said forces organized against it.[72] As Beale says,

> Hence, the "ruling and subduing" of Genesis 1:28 now includes spiritually overcoming the influence of evil in the hearts of unregenerate humanity that has multiplied upon earth. The implication is that the notion of physical newborn children "increasing and multiplying" in the original Genesis 1:28 commission now includes people who have left their old way of life and have become spiritually newborn and have come to reflect the image of God's glorious presence and participate in the expanding nature of the Genesis 1:26–28 commission.[73]

In short, the "ruling and subduing" is a ruling and reigning over a renewed earth; this is where the kingdom of God and new creation intersect, and both find their conceptual beginnings in Genesis 1:28. The kingdom of God is the rule over the new creation. In fact, the image of God at creation expresses "Adamic kingship," which functions as a divine status necessary

---

70. Beale, *New Testament Biblical Theology*, 87.
71. Beale, *New Testament Biblical Theology*, 42.
72. Beale, *New Testament Biblical Theology*, 53.
73. Beale, *New Testament Biblical Theology*, 53.

Inaugurated Eschatology and the Two-Ages Model

to fulfill the original commission. Beale gives an example from the ancient Near East where he says, for instance,

> ... King Assurbanipal affirms that the gods "gave me a splendid figure and made my strength great." And to be in the image of god meant that the king reflected god's glory. Thus, ancient Near Eastern kings being said to be in the image of their gods was part of "the institution of kingship itself, giving concrete form to underlying concepts of divinity sanctioned rule and ideal qualities of the ruler. Therefore, the king as the image of God was understood as a royal figure who "represents the god by virtue of his royal office and portrayed as acting like the god in specific behavioral ways.[74]

This functional definition does not preclude an ontological definition of the *imago Dei*.[75] The ontological is in addition to a functional definition. It seems logical to say the functional (God's vicegerent) presupposes the ontological; that is, Adam was a volitional, rational, moral agent/creature who reflected God's volitional, rational, moral agency as Creator. The ontological made it possible for Adam to function as the divine vicegerent.[76] Hoekema says, "the image of God is the key to man's identity; in other words, man is a representative of what it means to be in the image of God."[77] In short, man as vicegerent represents God to function in the role as king. Kolawole insightfully connects the ontological with the functional when he says,

> The mental likeness has to do with the intellect of man. Thus, the ability to know and communicate with God who is a rational being makes man a rational being. As a result, man (Adam) was given responsibilities that only rational beings could perform; they include: to work and take care of the garden (Gen 2:15), to rule over all creations (Gen 1:26–28), to name all animals (Gen 2:19–20). Far beyond that Adam recognized his wife as a helper suitable for him (Gen 2:22). The fact remains that only an intellectual and a mentally inclined being can perform and be saddled with these responsibilities.[78]

---

74. Beale, *New Testament Biblical Theology*, 31.
75. More will be said on this point below in my last chapter.
76. John Piper argues that there is both strengths and weaknesses with both a functional and ontological definition of the Imago Dei. He prefers the latter over the former. See Piper, "Image of God."
77. Hoekema, *Created in God's Image*, 264.
78. Kolawole, "God's Image in Man," 45–46.

Kingdom Theology

In short, the intellectual/mental (ontological) aspect of the *imago Dei* makes it possible for man to perform and be responsible (functional) as God's kingly vicegerent. This is the relationship between the kingdom of God and new creation as new-creational reign.

In light of this notion of the resurrection as the inauguration of both the kingdom of God and new creation, is there exegetical evidence for what Beale calls the new-creational reign of Christ—the complex of resurrection (new creation) and the kingdom of God? Below I will point to the Gospel of John and Acts, but first let me define what Beale means by new-creational reign. For Beale there are three senses for new-creational reign:

> [First] Is it employed with the strict idea of specific apocalyptic notion of the dissolution and re-creation of the entire cosmos, including the resurrection of people? [Second] Or does it function as a theological construct in which all eschatological hopes are wrapped up in one theological package? [Third] Or does it allude to the general future hope, typical of Israel's worldview in which the following are included as the objects of that hope: resurrection, renewal of the cosmos, vindication of Israel, return from captivity, salvation among those believing among the nations, punishment of the wicked nations, and, possibly, other theological themes that need to be linked together? My answer is that I am using the phrase "new-creational reign" broadly with all three senses and thus to refer to the entire network of ideas that belong to renewal of the whole world of Israel, and of the individual.[79]

The inauguration of the new-creational reign of Christ began with Christ's life, death, resurrection, and Christ's ongoing ascended reign in heaven, especially as it pertains to our Lord's resurrection. The reason is because the resurrection both of Christ and of the saints are the "mode of participation," marking not only the beginning of new creation but the manner by which Christ and the elect saints participate in the new creation.[80] There is no doubt that the Gospels, and especially the Gospel of John, teach that the end of the age will culminate with the physical resurrection of the dead:

> Truly, truly, I say to you, whoever hears my word and believes him who sent me has eternal life. He does not come into judgment, but has passed from death to life. "Truly, truly, I say to you, an hour is coming, and is now here, when the dead will hear the voice of the Son of God, and those who hear will live. For as the Father has life

79. Beale, *New Testament Biblical Theology*, 178.
80. Beale, *New Testament Biblical Theology*, 227.

> in himself, so he has granted the Son also to have life in himself. And he has given him authority to execute judgment, because he is the Son of Man. Do not marvel at this, for an hour is coming when all who are in the tombs will hear his voice and come out, those who have done good to the resurrection of life, and those who have done evil to the resurrection of judgment. (John 5:24–29)

What's striking about this pericope is Jesus' teaching that at the end of this present evil age there will be not only a general, physical, bodily resurrection of the wicked and righteous, but also a present, spiritual resurrection that has "already" been inaugurated. D. A. Carson sees in John 5:24 a case in point of the "strongest affirmation of inaugurated eschatology."[81] Also, the notions of new creation and resurrection are equated to the "kingdom of God" in John 3:1–15. The phrase "see/enter the kingdom of God" in verses 3 and 5 is a participation in the kingdom by means of experiencing eternal resurrected life in verse 15. The reason for this connection is because the idea of being "born again" is ". . . likely tied to the OT concept of resurrection and thus new creation."[82] Jesus' skeptical reply to Nicodemus' not understanding the notion of being born again is telling. Why does Jesus expect Nicodemus to have understood what he was teaching? As Beale convincingly argues, Ezekiel 36:25–27 is the only Old Testament text that connects end-time renewal with "water" and "Spirit."[83] Also, Ezekiel 36 is parallel to Ezekiel 37, which is a pictorial portrayal of Israel's return from exile and a prediction of the resurrection.[84] Jesus' reference to being "born of water and Spirit" is an allusion to Ezekiel 36, an allusion that Jesus expected Nicodemus to have known. In this context "Jesus appropriately terms the resurrection/new creation of the prophecy in Ezekiel 36 as being 'born again.'"[85]

Another example of the new-creational reign of Christ is in Acts 1. More will be said regarding this below, but suffice to say Acts 1:1–11 is an expansion on the Lukan ending in Luke 24:46–51. In Acts 1:6 the disciples ask, "Is it at this time you are restoring the kingdom of Israel?" In response, Jesus connects his resurrection ministry with the kingdom of God. As P. W. L. Walker says, "Israel was being restored through the resurrection of

---

81. Carson, *Gospel According to John*, 256.
82. Beale, *New Testament Biblical Theology*, 234.
83. Beale, *New Testament Biblical Theology*, 234..
84. Beale, *New Testament Biblical Theology*, 236.
85. Beale, *New Testament Biblical Theology*, 236.

its Messiah and the forthcoming gift of the Spirit," that is, the restoration of Israel as the church made up of regenerate Jews and gentiles.[86] Beale observes that the difference between Jesus' commencement of his kingdom during his life and ministry located in Capernaum vs. his resurrection and ascension has more to do with the escalation of the kingdom, that Jesus' resurrection and ascension are an escalation of the kingdom that he had commenced in his pre-resurrection condition.[87] This is why Beale rightly says that the "NT eschatological center of gravity has moved from the earthly realm (in the Gospels) to the heavenly realm (in Acts and Paul)." This notion of the restoration of the kingdom is taken up in Peter's sermon in Acts 2:22–36, where Peter makes two points: first, Christ's resurrection is a "loosing [of] the pangs of death" in verse 24, and second, the resurrection fulfills the promise to David to "set one of his descendants on his throne" in verses 30–31.

In Acts 13 it's Paul who preaches a similar sermon as did Peter in Acts 2. In Acts 13:33 Paul asserts that it was at the point of Christ's resurrection in fulfillment of Old Testament prophecy that Christ was installed as Messiah: "God has fulfilled this promise to our children in that He raised up Jesus, as it is also written in the second Psalm, 'You are My son; today I have begotten you.'" Beale summarizes these two sermons from Acts 2 and 13 as such:

> Thus, in the two structurally crucial sermons in Acts 2 and Acts 13 the concepts of new creation through resurrection from de-creation of death and of kingdom establishment through resurrection are very closely linked, which is especially highlighted by repeated mention of the resurrection of the Messiah (i.e., the eschatological Israelite king) in the Acts 2 account. Therefore, the idea of the new-creational kingdom is underscored by explaining Jesus's resurrection from the dead.[88]

In short, the new-creational reign of Christ entails Christ's kingship, that is, Jesus' role of vicegerency over new creation, a new creation inaugurated by means of the resurrection. This new creation is the realm or divine order of the kingdom of God; and the age to come is the eternal time of new creation.

---

86. Walker, *Jesus and the Holy City*, 292.
87. Beale, *New Testament Biblical Theology*, 238.
88. Beale, *New Testament Biblical Theology*, 240.

The Sign of the Eschaton: The Descent of the Holy Spirit on the Church

This takes me to the second focus of the Eschaton, that is, the descent of the Holy Spirit on the church. It is common knowledge among biblical scholars that the Gospels (for example, John 2:19–22) teach that Jesus recognized that he was the end-time eschatological temple, as well as the New Testament's witness that the visible church is too the end-time eschatological temple or "temple of the Holy Spirit" (for example, 2 Cor 6:16). However, there is no explicit mention of the precise genesis of the church as the end-time eschatological temple. When was the end-time eschatological temple inaugurated? The end-time eschatological temple was inaugurated at Pentecost, launched by Christ's resurrection, ascension, and enthronement; Christ sent the Spirit to continue to build the end-time eschatological temple at Pentecost.

Christ as the End-Time Temple

Before I say more about the genesis of the end-time temple, let me say a bit more about Jesus as the new end-time temple. Apart from explicit statements where Jesus asserts that he is the end-time temple, others are implicit. Case in point: in Luke 7:49–50 Jesus states that he can forgive sin. This is one of many statements where Jesus claims this divine prerogative. This is why, in part, the religious leaders accused him of blasphemy (for example, Matt 9:3), which underscores said divine prerogative. This strongly implies temple identification, because one major function of the temple was sacrifices for the forgiveness of sins. The temple was the divinely instituted sacred location where forgiveness was dispensed. Now, Jesus has become the divinely instituted location where forgiveness is found because "the Son of Man has authority on earth to forgive sins" (Matt 9:2–6). Also, in Matthew 12:6 Jesus identifies himself as "something greater than the temple." Why? "God's presence is more manifest in Him than in the Temple. On Him, not the Temple, rests the 'Shekinah' glory."[89] This echoes Haggai 2:9, where the prophet says that the "latter glory of this house will be greater than the former." Jesus is the "latter glory," that is to say, the unique presence of the glory of God manifested in a greater way than at an architectural temple. In short, the witness of Scripture is that Jesus is the temple for two reasons.

---

89. Cole, *New Temple*, 12.

First, Jesus is the embodiment of the glory of God's presence. The temple represented the presence of God being with man. Jesus as the God-man by virtue of his personage is the presence of God being with man. Second, Jesus embodies the way to the presence of God. Just as the temple is the gate to God's presence by means of sacrifices; likewise Jesus is the gate to God's presence by way of his atoning death. Clowney says it this way:

> We have seen that the altar at the gate is essential to the symbolism of the tabernacle. Without an offering for sin God cannot dwell among sinners, nor can they enter his courts to worship. Christ provides not only the glory of God's presence but the way of approach into God's presence, the altar at the gate of God. When the glory of God tabernacles among men, then his prophet cries, "Behold the Lamb of God that taketh away the sin of the world!" (John 1:29). . . . All that the temple means, then, is fulfilled in Jesus Christ: the dwelling of God's glory in the sanctuary; the provision of atoning sacrifice at the gate; the meeting of fellowship where the praises and prayers of Israel ascend from the holy feast; the flowing water of life that comes forth from the threshold of the house—all are realities in Christ.[90]

Also, the temple was supposed to have been a place to be a witness to the nations, not a superstitious symbol of Jewish ethnocentrism. In part, this is why Jesus cleansed the temple in Matthew 21:12–13 and parallel accounts in Mark 11:15–19 and Luke 19:45–48. As N. T. Wright notes, Jesus' act of cleansing the temple was an act of judgement not only because of its misuse but also because the temple represented Israel's rejection of God's Word and Jesus himself.[91] Jesus quotes Isaiah 56:3–8; in context Isaiah is prophesying that the temple in the latter days will become a location where the gentiles will come as a place to pray. Jesus is judging the temple because it's not fulfilling its said role; it "was not fulfilling its God-ordained role as a witness to the nations but has become, like the first temple, the premier symbol of a superstitious belief that God would protect and rally his people irrespective of their conformity to his will."[92]

---

90. Clowney, "Final Temple," 175–78.
91. N. T. Wright, *Jesus and the Victory of God*, 413–27.
92. Carson, "Matthew," 442.

Inaugurated Eschatology and the Two-Ages Model

The Church as the End-Time Temple

It's clear from Scripture that Christ is the embodiment of the end-time temple. However, what's the connection between Christ as the temple and his church being the temple? Edmund Clowney says,

> Precisely because Christ builds the temple in himself, he can build it in his disciples. The significance of the temple symbol is the reality it symbolized: the dwelling of God in the midst of his people and their gathering together to meet with him. Christ builds the temple in himself as he actualizes the saving presence of God. Christ builds the temple in his people as he gathers them to himself.[93]

Clowney argues that Christ builds the temple in his people the church as he gathers them to himself. This connection between Christ as the end-time temple and the church as the end-time temple is based on two principles. He says,

> It is because Christ is the real temple in his death and resurrection that the church, and individual Christians as well, can be described as temples of God. This follows from two principles that are drawn together in the Pauline formula "in Christ." The first is the fact that by being united to Christ, Christians share in the realities Christ has accomplished. Those who are joined to Christ are raised from the dead with him and are therefore made with him the New Temple of God. The other principle is that those who are united to Christ have him not only as their representative — the new Adam heading a new mankind; they have him also as their life. The last Adam is not merely a living soul as was the first (Gen. 2:7), he is a life-giving Spirit (I Cor. 15:45). Christians are made to be temples because the Spirit of Christ dwells in them; the church is a temple because it is the Spirit-indwelt body of Christ.[94]

What are some explicit biblical texts that demonstrate that the church is the end-time temple? According to Ephesians, believers are "built on the foundation of the apostles and prophets, Christ Jesus himself being the cornerstone, in whom the whole structure, being joined together, grows into a holy temple in the Lord. In him you also are being built together into a dwelling place for God by the Spirit" (Eph 2:20–22). It's patently clear that

---

93. Clowney, "Final Temple," 173.
94. Clowney, "Final Temple," 184–85.

Christians are identified with Christ as the temple, growing and expanding as the dwelling place of God here on earth. As Clowney says,

> The redeemed are one in Christ's body; they are one body in Christ (Rom. 12:5); they are a body of Christ (without the article: I Cor. 12:27); they are the body of Christ (Eph. 4:12). The church's existence as the body-temple depends totally on the resurrection body of Christ in which the church is raised up, and on the Spirit of Christ by which the church lives. Paul's appeals for the unity of the church are drawn from the unity of the body of Christ as the true and final temple. For Paul the body and the temple go together: the breaking down of the middle wall of the temple creates one body; the New Temple grows as a body (Eph. 2:21); the body is built as a temple (Eph. 4:12, 16), Christ is the cornerstone of the structure, the Lord in whom the New Temple exists.[95]

The question is this: is the language of the temple metaphorical or actual, actual in that the church is the inaugurated fulfillment of Old Testament expectations of an end-time temple? Some scholars see such language as metaphorical rather than actually a redemptive-historical fulfillment of Israel's prophecies concerning the end-time temple.[96] Others consider such language as a spiritualizing of the Old by the New Testament authors.[97] This will depend upon whether New Testament texts explicitly cite supporting Old Testament texts to make the point of Old Testament fulfillment of end-time temple prophecies.

---

95. Clowney, "Final Temple," 184–85.
96. Levison, "Spirit and the Temple."
97. See Clowney, "Final Temple," 182–83. Clowney highlights the "spiritualization" during the Hellenistic era. He says, "Demythologizing was in the air in the Hellenistic Age. The pagan myths had been rehabilitated as philosophical allegories. Philo had used this method to present the Old Testament to the Alexandrian intellectual.... When we find Christians described as the living stones of a new temple, when their benevolent gifts are 'an odor of a sweet smell, a sacrifice acceptable, well-pleasing to God' (Phil. 4:18), when their bodies are spoken of as temples of the Holy Spirit, then it might seem that the cult has been spiritualized by transposing into figurative language what was once symbolic action." He notes that this is not the case for the New Testament authors. He says, "Our reflection on the claims of Christ has already shown us that the use of the Old Testament is far from figurative. The situation is completely reversed. In the wisdom of God's purpose, the earlier revelation points forward to the climax, when, in the fullness of time, God sent his own Son into the world. Christ is the true temple, the true light of glory, the true manna, the true vine. The coming of the true supersedes the figurative. The veil of the temple made with hands is destroyed, for its symbolism is fulfilled."

INAUGURATED ESCHATOLOGY AND THE TWO-AGES MODEL

Does Ephesians 2:19–22 demonstrate Old Testament support for New Testament inaugurated fulfillment? The context of Ephesians 2 strongly suggests, in Paul's thinking, that the church is in reality a redemptive historical fulfillment of Israel's fulfillment of end-time temple prophecies, that the church in its inaugurated form is the end-time temple. In verse 17 Paul quotes a restoration prophesy from Isaiah 57:19, where Paul says, "And he came and preached peace to you who were far off and peace to those who were near" (Eph 2:17). Why does Paul quote this? Paul quotes it to support his preceding point: that is, by virtue of Christ's death and resurrection, both Jews and gentiles are reconciled to God; Christ's resurrection has created a new, eschatological humanity called the church. This reconciliation to God by means of Christ's resurrection is only possible because both Jew and gentile are one in Christ. Because of their oneness in Christ and their reconciliation with God, Jews and gentiles are at peace with one another. This one qualitatively new (καινός) man, in contradistinction to the old humanity of Jew and gentile, transcends all nationalistic identities. What used to alienate Jews and gentiles (that is, ethnic and nationalistic and tribal identities) are nugatory.

This is what Paul means in Galatians when he says, ". . . neither circumcision nor uncircumcision is anything, but a new creation" (Gal 6:15). Circumcision is as nugatory as uncircumcision in identifying the people of God. Only new creation by grace in Christ marks a person a member of the household (temple) of God. It's here that Paul introduces the phrase "Israel of God": "And as many as walk according to this rule, peace and mercy *be* upon them, and upon the Israel of God" (Gal 6:16). Paul pronounces a blessing (his apostolic approval) on those who abide by this rule of conduct. What rule? The rule of conduct that asserts that no distinction is to be made to identify between the circumcised (that is, Jews) and the uncircumcised (that is, gentiles) people of God, that ethnic and national identity (that is, Jewishness by means of ceremonial circumcision) do not identify the people of God. The people of God are distinguished by the inward mark of faith, not the outward mark of ethnicity and/or national identity. In short, the people of God (that is, the church made up of Jews and gentiles who live by the rule of no outward marks of ethnic or national distinction) are the "Israel of God," precluding the nation of Israel as the Israel of God.[98]

---

98. See Robertson, *Israel of God*, 41–46. Robertson posits three interpretations. The first is to interpret *kai* simply as "and," in which case Paul would be pronouncing his blessing on two groups or categories of people: those who do recognize this rule ("as many as") of making no distinction between Jews and gentiles, on the one hand, and on

In both contexts (Gal 6 and Eph 2), ethnic and nationalistic and tribal identities are null and void as outward marks of the new eschatological humanity, that is, the church. The church (believing Jews and gentiles in Christ) is part of Christ and is a new creation in him according to Ephesians 2. And because of this, believing Jews and gentiles are part of the "one Spirit," having open "access" to the Father (Eph 2:3). This access is interpreted by Paul in Eph 2:19–22 as being the temple of God of which Christ is the "cornerstone." If Christ as the temple refers to Christ as the fulfillment of Old Testament prophesies regarding the end-time eschatological temple, then Christ as cornerstone is Christ functioning as the foundation stone for the temple as church. Christ is the cornerstone by virtue of his death and resurrection. The church's building project began when the foundation was laid; the laying of the foundation was during the apostolic age of the New Testament apostles and prophets. The images depicted in the context of Ephesians 2—for example, images of being "in Christ," "in one new man," "in one Spirit," and "into a holy temple—are one and the same reality, a reality that exists in the presence of God. Isaiah 57:19 in context is about returning from exile and restoration in terms of dwelling in God's temple.[99] In short, Paul refers to Isaiah 57 in relation to the temple and the promise of returning to a restored end-time temple.

Another explicit reference (Beale contends the most explicit[100]) regarding believers being identified as the end-time temple is 2 Corinthians 6:16. Paul says, "For we are the temple of the living God." Paul combines both Leviticus and Ezekiel as a prediction of the end-time temple to come.

---

the other hand, another group, i.e., "the Israel of God," who do hold to this distinction. He correctly notes that though this is grammatically plausible, it is not contextually possible because Paul would not approve of what he just disapproved of in his argument. Another interpretation is to take *kai* epexegetically: the "as many as" are explained to be the Israel of God who are believing Jews, i.e., believing Jews who hold to this rule of no distinction. In this sense "the Israel of God" would mean (what we would say today) messianic Jews. This is inadequate because it's too minimalistic, i.e., messianic Jews are not the only ones who hold to this rule. In context Paul approves of both believing Jews and gentiles who live by this rule of no distinction. The third interpretation is the only acceptable one, both grammatically (epexegetically) and contextually: that is, Paul is speaking of one group of people, i.e., the church made up of believing Jews and gentiles, who abides by Paul's rule of no distinction as being "the Israel of God."

99. Beale, *New Testament Biblical Theology*, 726. Beale makes the point that Isa 57:19 is a prophesy about Israel's restoration, not the gentile nations. The point is that both gentile and Jewish believers are "viewed as being restored as end-time Israel," which includes the end-time temple.

100. Beale, *New Testament Biblical Theology*, 635.

Inaugurated Eschatology and the Two-Ages Model

Leviticus says, "I will make my dwelling among you, and my soul shall not abhor you. And I will walk among you and will be your God, and you shall be my people. (Lev 26:11–12). And Ezekiel says,

> I will make a covenant of peace with them. It shall be an everlasting covenant with them. And I will set them in their land and multiply them, and will set my sanctuary in their midst forevermore. My dwelling place shall be with them, and I will be their God, and they shall be my people, (Ezek 37:26–27)

Paul alludes to both of these prophecies: "I will make my dwelling among them and walk among them, and I will be their God, and they shall be my people" (2 Cor 6:16b). Paul is not making a mere analogy between the church, on the one hand, and the temple, on the other hand. Paul takes this to be a prediction of the coming end-time temple. Christians (both individually and corporately) are the inaugurated fulfillment of said prophecy.[101] Clowney nicely summarizes 2 Corinthians 6 this way:

> But is Paul only borrowing language? Ezekiel prophesies in the name of the Lord, "I will set my sanctuary in the midst of them forevermore. My tabernacle also shall be with them; and I will be their God, and they shall be my people..." (Ezek. 37:26b, 27). Paul responds, "... we are a temple of the living God; even as God said, I will dwell in them, and walk in them; and I will be their God, and they shall be my people" (II Cor. 6:16). No, God who has become our Father and made us sons and daughters in Jesus Christ — the living God has given us with unveiled face to behold his glory in the face of Jesus Christ (II Cor. 3:18).... Do not propose to the Apostle Paul that God's holy sanctuary of the last days, begun in the Spirit, will be completed in the flesh! The temple which Ezekiel prophesied is the temple of the covenant, of God's presence claiming his people forever. The Apostle labored as a master builder in that temple, working in gold, silver, and precious stones, laying no other foundation than the one which God set in place, Jesus

---

101. See Clowney, "Final Temple," 185. He notes, "The redeemed are one in Christ's body; they are one body in Christ (Rom. 12:5); they are a body of Christ (without the article: I Cor. 12:27); they are the body of Christ (Eph. 4:12). The church's existence as the body-temple depends totally on the resurrection body of Christ in which the church is raised up, and on the Spirit of Christ by which the church lives. Paul's appeals for the unity of the church are drawn from the unity of the body of Christ as the true and final temple. For Paul the body and the temple go together: the breaking down of the middle wall of the temple creates one body; the New Temple grows as a body (Eph. 2:21); the body is built as a temple (Eph. 4:12, 16), Christ is the cornerstone of the structure, the Lord in whom the New Temple exists."

Christ. No, Paul is not borrowing figurative language. He is proclaiming spiritual realities—dimly perceived when the first son of David summoned workmen from Tyre, but abundantly fulfilled when the last son of David formed the eternal place of meeting in the temple not made with hands. When we view the glory of the spiritual temple of the of the New Covenant, it would seem that no further heightening is possible. The true Son of David and true Son of God has come. All that the temple is fulfilled in him and in his people. The Gentiles are brought in and the temple of living stones grows in glory and holiness.[102]

The Eschatological Genesis of the End-Time Temple

Back to the question of the genesis of the end-time temple, there is no explicit mention of the precise genesis of the church as the end-time eschatological temple. As Beale says, "there is no explicit mention of the decisive time when the Church was first founded as the eschatological temple."[103] When was the end-time eschatological temple inaugurated? Matthew, Mark, and John all mention Israel's temple being replaced by Christ rebuilding a new temple by his resurrection, in contradistinction to Luke, who doesn't mention Christ being the replacement of the temple.[104]

Beale argues that the end-time eschatological temple was inaugurated at Pentecost, launched by virtue of Christ's resurrection, ascension, and enthronement; Christ sent the Spirit to continue to build the end-time eschatological temple at Pentecost. Beale makes the case that though the word "temple" is not used in Acts 2 the concept, nonetheless, of "the descending heavenly temple" is there.[105] It is Beale's contention that "God's heavenly tabernacle and theophanic presence" came down in the form of the Spirit, "extending the heavenly temple down to earth to include his people in it by building them into it."[106]

---

102. Clowney, "Final Temple," 186–87.
103. Beale, "Descent of the Eschatological Temple," 73.
104. Beale, "Descent of the Eschatological Temple," 74.
105. Beale, "Descent of the Eschatological Temple," 74.
106. Beale, "Descent of the Eschatological Temple," 74. To bolster his point Beale points to the fact that many Old Testament texts regarding the end-time temple will be a non-architectural temple (e.g., Isa 4:2–6; 30:27–30; Jer 3:16–17; Zech 1:16—2:13; cf. Ezek 40–46).

What is the evidence? What follows is Beale's most convincing evidence. Beale first looks at the connection between Pentecost and Babel. It's well known that many scholars believe that the tongues at Pentecost are best seen against the backdrop of the tower of Babel. As God judged Babel by dividing their language into languages because they attempted to unite the masses to build a temple-tower to force God to condescend to bless the people, in contradistinction, God reverses the curse of Babel at Pentecost by causing the nations to hear the same message in their native language as though the languages were one language. The curse at Babel is reversed by the blessing at Pentecost.

Many see the tongues at Pentecost as connected to the tower of Babel. What Beale adds is that he sees a temple background to Babel, that the tower of Babel was a temple-tower, that is, ". . . its cultic import may be to set in contrast to the new temple that emerges along with the phenomenon of tongues, which now has been transformed into blessing."[107] In short, the temple-tower[108] of Babel is set in contrast to the emergence of the new temple at Pentecost.

Second, Beale looks to Sinai as a temple-sanctuary and sees this as a background to Pentecost. Beale remarks on the phenomenon of "tongues of fire." "Tongues of fire" is well understood by most scholars as being an expression of the presence of God by means of a theophany. This theophanic presence expresses the coming of the Spirit. However, Beale says that there is more: "It appears to be a theophany associated with the descending divine presence of the heavenly temple."[109] A few things need to be considered. First, when Acts 2 describes Pentecost as "a noise like a violent, rushing wind" and "tongues of fire" appearing, Beale observes that this is an allusion to "typical theophanies of the Old Testament." He says the "first great theophany of the Old Testament was at Sinai, where 'God descended on it in fire' and appeared in the midst of loud 'voices and torches and a thick cloud' and 'fire' . . ."[110] Sinai typified and modeled similar divine theophanic appearances in later Old Testament salvation history,

---

107. Beale, "Descent of the Eschatological Temple," 76.

108. Beale, "Descent of the Eschatological Temple," 75. Beale notes that cultic towers were typical in ancient Mesopotamia, serving as a "gateway between heaven and earth."

109. Beale, "Descent of the Eschatological Temple," 76.

110. Beale, "Descent of the Eschatological Temple," 76.

"... making God's coming at Sinai [stand] in the background of the Spirit's coming at Pentecost."[111]

Beale concedes that though Luke's account of Pentecost may contain no direct cross references from the "Sinai theophany," he does give examples of "indirect allusions" that indicate that Luke was cognizant of Sinai as a background to his portrayal of Pentecost. What are some of his biblical examples? First, he points to the unanimity and oneness of spirit the people experienced at the same sacred location. For example, Exodus 19:8 reads, "All the people answered together and said, 'All that the Lord has spoken we will do.' And Moses reported the words of the people to the Lord." Acts 1:14 reads, "All these with one accord were devoting themselves to prayer, together with the women and Mary the mother of Jesus, and his brothers." Acts 2:1–2 reads, "When the day of Pentecost arrived, they were all together in one place. And suddenly there came from heaven a sound like a mighty rushing wind, and it filled the entire house where they were sitting." Second, he correlates the sounds that "came from heaven" at Sinai (for example, Exod 20:22 and Deut 4:36) to the sounds from heaven at Pentecost in Acts 2:2. Third, in general, just as Moses' ascension directly preceded Sinai's theophanic revelation, likewise Jesus' ascension directly preceded Pentecost's theophanic revelation.[112] In particular he points to Moses' two forty-day periods of time where he stays on top of Mount Sinai, and Jesus' forty-day post-resurrection experience. Another is just as Moses entered the cloud at Mount Sinai as he ascended in Exodus 24:15–18, likewise Jesus' ascension occurred on a mountain as he ascended in a cloud from the sight of his disciples (see Acts 1:11–12; cf. Luke 24:50.) Beale notes that these "... parallels suggest that Luke was intending to some degree that his readers have in mind God's revelation to Moses at Sinai as a backdrop to understanding the events leading up to and climaxing at Pentecost."[113]

Third, after presenting these lines that suggest a strong "probability" in favor of a Sinai-Pentecost identification, Beale compares Pentecost's image of speech with the image of speech in the midst of fire as "tongues of fire" in the Old Testament as a theophany from God's heavenly sanctuary.[114] Isaiah 30:27–30 refers to God as "descending" from his heavenly temple. Isaiah 30:27–30 is one of two places in the Old Testament where

---

111. Beale, "Descent of the Eschatological Temple," 77.
112. Beale, "Descent of the Eschatological Temple," 81.
113. Beale, "Descent of the Eschatological Temple," 82.
114. Beale, "Descent of the Eschatological Temple," 84.

the phrase "tongues as of fire" is mentioned. Niehaus is correct to say that Isaiah 30:27–30 is a clear allusion to the prototypical theophany of Sinai.[115] This theophany from Isaiah 30 is directly connected with the "mountain of the Lord" at Sinai. Beale notices the significance of this because the same expression "the mountain of the Lord" in Isaiah 2:3 refers to the eschatological temple. Another location where "tongues of fire" is located is Isaiah 5:24–25. In context Isaiah 5 is emblematic of judgment, a scene of judgment from the heavenly temple like Isaiah 30.[116] Other texts in addition to Isaiah are Psalm 18:3, where God's fiery word comes from his heavenly temple, and Psalm 29:7, where the voice of God "flashes forth flames of fire" from his temple. This motif of judgment in relation to flames of tongues is also alluded to in 1 Corinthians 14:21–22, where Paul teaches that tongues are a sign, in part, of judgment against unbelieving Jews.

Fourth, Beale points to Peter's Old Testament quotation from Joel 2:28–29 and Isaiah 2:2 as a fulfillment of Acts 2:1–12. Peter quotes Joel 2 as an initial fulfillment at Pentecost in that God "pour[s] out" his "Spirit upon all flesh." Beale notices that Peter substitutes the phrase "after these things" in Joel 2 with "in the latter day." Why the substitution? "In the latter day" is taken from Isaiah 2:2, the only place in the Septuagint where this precise phrase occurs. Isaiah 2 is predicting the future inauguration of the end-time temple, when the nation will come under its influence. Peter seems to be interpreting Joel as the initial fulfillment of the Spirit's coming at Pentecost as the end-time temple upon God's people, on the one hand, and, on the other hand. emphasizing the Spirit bestowing God's gifts to the people of God. The latter is also associated with the temple in the context of priests being bestowed with spiritual gifts to function as priest in the temple.

In the Old Testament dispensation, only priests, prophets, and kings were bestowed with spiritual gifts to serve in conjunction with the temple. Both Joel 2 and Acts 2 emphasize the function of the Spirit, not in regeneration, but in enabling to serve in various capacities though regeneration is presupposed. Joel foresaw a time when everyone in Israel would be gifted with spiritual gifts. When Peter quotes Joel, while substituting the phrase "in the latter day" from Isaiah 2:2, Beale observes that this is strong evidence that Acts 2 and Joel 2 have in mind supernatural gifting in service of the new end-time temple. As Dillard observes, this connection with Joel 2 and Acts 2 with the end-time temple is apparent in that Joel's prophesy

---

115. Niehaus, *God at Sinai*, 307–8.
116. Beale, "Descent of the Eschatological Temple," 85.

Kingdom Theology

is a development from the Numbers 11.[117] In Numbers 11:1—12:8 Moses is burdened and desires that God would give him help to lead the people (11:11, 17). In response to this, God tells Moses to gather seventy men from the elder leadership and bring them to the tabernacle to stand there. Then God promises that he will take the Spirit upon Moses and will place the Spirit upon the seventy elders (see 11:16–17). Moses does as he's commanded:

> So Moses went out and told the people the words of the Lord. And he gathered seventy men of the elders of the people and placed them around the tent. Then the Lord came down in the cloud and spoke to him, and took some of the Spirit that was on him and put it on the seventy elders. And as soon as the Spirit rested on them, they prophesied. But they did not continue doing it. (Num 11:24–25)

The elders stopped prophesying; however, two elders at a near location continued prophesying. Joshua overhears these two elders prophesying, and out of zeal for Moses' position of leadership, he asks Moses to stop them from prophesying. Moses' response is this: "'Are you jealous for my sake? Would that all the Lord's people were prophets, that the Lord would put his Spirit on them!' And Moses and the elders of Israel returned to the camp" (Num 11:29–30). Beale calls Moses' request a "prophetic wish," a prophetic wish that became a "formal prophesy" in Joel 2.[118] Peter quotes Joel 2 to show that Pentecost is the inaugural fulfillment of Joel's prophesy that Moses' prophetic wish is coming to fruition. Peter quotes Joel's prophesy to demonstrate that Pentecost is the inaugurated fulfillment of Joel 2. The point is this: "The Spirit's gifting, formally limited to leaders helping Moses and imparted to them at the tabernacle, is universalized to all of God's people from every race, young and old, male and female."[119] And just as in Numbers 11, which observes that the "seventy elders" received the Spirit as they gathered around the tabernacle, likewise the Spirit's gifting in Acts 2 of the 120 who gathered are the end-time temple.

Another allusion is observed in Numbers 11:25. It notes that God took the Spirit who was upon Moses and placed the Spirit upon the seventy elders. In comparison, in Acts 2:33, Jesus had first received from the Father the promise of the Holy Spirit, and then later the Spirit was "poured forth"

---

117. Dillard, "Intrabiblical Exegesis," 90.
118. Beale, "Descent of the Eschatological Temple," 95.
119. Beale, "Descent of the Eschatological Temple," 95.

upon the 120 at Pentecost, making Jesus a second Moses.[120] In short, Beale makes a convincing argument that dates Pentecost as the genesis of the church being the end-time temple.

The Church as the End-Time Manifestation of the Reign of God

Last, but not least, is the relationship between the church and the kingdom of God. If the church is the end-time redemptive presence of God as temple, then it seems reasonable to conclude that the church is the end-time redemptive rule of God made manifest in this present age. In what sense is the church the manifestation of the kingdom of God in this age?

The two pivotal texts of Scripture evincing the church as the manifestation of the kingdom of God are Matthew 16 and 18. Much ink has been spilt expounding both these texts and the meaning of the "keys," but I will limit my comments to the connection between the church and the kingdom. In Matthew 16:16–18, Jesus teaches on the founding of the church. The church is founded "upon the rock" of Peter's confession that Jesus is "the Christ, the son of the living God." Jesus then says in verse 19, "I will give you the keys of the kingdom of heaven, and whatever you bind on earth shall be bound in heaven, and whatever you loose on earth shall be loosed in heaven." In Matthew 18 it is clear that when Jesus says "you," he does not mean Peter. It's not to Peter Jesus is handing over the keys of the kingdom, but to the church as represented by all twelve disciples, that is, the church as represented by her officers; it's the officers of the church who are given the keys to the kingdom. The keys of the kingdom are simply the authority of the kingdom, the right to act in king Jesus' name. The right to exercise kingdom authority is given neither to governments, nor to popes, nor to kings; it's given to the visible, institutional church. In short, the relationship between the church and the kingdom of God is that the church is an embassy or outpost of the kingdom of God, manifesting God's rule by binding and loosing, that is, by preaching and teaching and church discipline. This is why Paul can say that through the church "the wisdom of God might now be known to the rulers and authorities in the heavenly places" (Eph 3:10). As Greg Gilbert says, ". . . the church is the primary arena God has chosen to make his redemptive reign over his people visible. It is, as some

---

120. Beale, "Descent of the Eschatological Temple," 96.

have said, the initial and exclusive manifestation of the kingdom of God in this age."[121]

CONCLUSION

In conclusion, God in Christ and through his church by virtue of the resurrection and descent of the Holy Spirit on the church has inaugurated both the eschatological kingdom and temple of God. Both the rule (that is, the kingdom inaugurated at Christ's resurrection) and presence (temple) of God are the two primary foci of the sign of the Eschaton, a sign that points to God's presence (temple) and present victorious reign (kingdom) in this present age. Eschatological victory is neither a future state of affairs beyond this age, as dispensationalists claim, nor a future golden period within this age, as some postmillennialists argue.[122] The present cultural dissidence in our age today does not contradict the current present reign of God in Christ. This present age will always be marked by evil and rebellion against Christ's kingdom rule and end-time temple presence, both instantiated in the church. An inaugurated notion of the kingdom of God denotes victory in this age (not merely a victory in the future at the end of this age), because Christ's death and resurrection inaugurated Christ's reign. Triumph in this age doesn't preclude tribulation but is constitutive of both tribulation and victory in this age.

The question before us is: how is the triumph of Christ's reign constitutive of both tribulation and victory? Is this a contradiction? Simply put,

---

121. DeYoung and Gilbert, *What Is the Mission*, 127.

122. Case in point for a reconstructionist, postmillennial view of eschatological victory as future cultural dominance and hegemony in this age is Gentry, "Whose Victory in History?," 215. He states: "The postmillennial conception of victory is of a progressive cultural victory and expansive influence of Christianity in history . . . . The personal status of the believer and the corporate standing of the Church in salvation is . . . one of present victory—in principle . . . . The distinctive postmillennial view of Christianity's progressive victory, in time and in history, into all of human life and culture, is postmillennialism's application of the doctrine of Christ's definitively completed salvation." Another example of this is North, *Millennialism and Social Theory*, 87. He says: "If neither we [Christians] nor our covenantal successors will ever be able in history to apply the Bible-specified sanctions of the heavenly King whom we represent on earth, then Christians cannot be said ever to reign in history. The language of reigning would then be both misleading and inappropriate. The issue here is simple: Christians' possession of the judicial authority to impose negative civil sanctions or the private economic power to impose both positive and negative cultural sanction" must be operative.

INAUGURATED ESCHATOLOGY AND THE TWO-AGES MODEL

it is categorically and unequivocally not a contradiction. It's a paradox. R. Fowler White points to what he calls the "irony of redemptive victory" to resolve the seeming antinomy between tribulation and victory.[123] The irony of redemptive victory is the means by which the seed would conquer the serpent. White points to Genesis 3:14–19, which provides the pattern of irony.[124] This, he says, is one of its most striking features of the "oracle of destiny." White says,

> God's curses here express the eschatologically significant moral principles by which he achieves victory over his enemies. God sees to it that the means by which his enemies would defeat him end up being the very means by which he defeats them; in addition, the actual results affected by God are the opposite to a greater degree of the results intended by his enemies. In Genesis 3, then, we find statements of retributive irony and redemptive irony.[125]

Regarding redemptive irony, there is gospel victory over the serpent. Through sin and deception on the part of the serpent, Satan was able to convert the woman, making her an ally and the mother of the serpent's wicked and perishing seed. In contradistinction, ironically, by the grace of God, God converts the "fallen women into an enemy of the serpent and into the mother of all righteous and living."[126] By sin the serpent made all the women's seed into the children of the devil. However, by grace "God determines to make a division among the woman's fallen seed, promising to convert a remnant into the children of God." Again, by sin the serpent subdues man, but by grace "God ordains that one son of the woman will subdue the serpent. By so much, God initiates the moral and spiritual conflict between the seed that will yet culminate in the fulfillment of God's original purpose for man."[127] The irony of redemptive victory is the means by which the seed will conquer the serpent. White says,

> By sin, the serpent had delivered man to the curses of death and defeat, hoping thereby to frustrate God's original commission to man. But God sees to it that the means by which the serpent and his seed intended to defeat him end up being the very means by which he defeats them; in addition, the actual results effected by

123. White, "Agony, Irony, and Victory," 171.
124. White, "Agony, Irony, and Victory," 170.
125. White, "Agony, Irony, and Victory," 170.
126. White, "Agony, Irony, and Victory," 170.
127. White, "Agony, Irony, and Victory," 171.

God are the opposite or a greater degree of the results intended by the serpent and his seed. By the grace of redemptive judgment, God appoints the death of one as the way to new life for many; he ordains the weak, even in death, to conquer the strong; he transforms curse into blessing. How can this be? Because in God's bittersweet sovereignty over the conflict, the one righteous seed will inflict suffering unto death (a head wound) on the serpent, as the serpent inflicts suffering unto death (a heel wound) on the woman's one righteous seed. Thus God promises that one of the woman's seed will succeed where Adam had failed: this last (eschatological) Adam will be victorious over the serpent where the first (protological) Adam had been defeated, and that victory will come by means of the curse of death.[128]

This ironic pattern of redemptive victory is the means by which Christ would conquer Satan at the cross. White says that this ironic pattern of redemptive, eschatological victory that we see in the "oracle of destiny"—aka the *protoevangelium*, what James August calls the "fountainhead of the Old Testament's anticipatory hope"[129]—culminates most strikingly in the book of Revelation. The language and images of victory are most prominent as John applies the language of victory to Christ and his people while employing this ironic pattern of victory from Genesis 3:15.

White points to how Christ is presented in Revelation. John presents Christ's redemption of the church in the imagery of a "new Exodus."[130] In Revelation 1:5–6, it is clear that John alludes to the Lord's work of redemption in the exodus, and compares that to Christ's redemptive work as the Lamb of God. Just as the Lord was victorious over Egypt by redeeming Israel at the Passover, likewise Christ as the anti-typical Passover Lamb is victorious over his enemies. This victory theme of Christ associated with Israel's Passover clearly took place at his death from John's reference to his

---

128. White, "Agony, Irony, and Victory," 171.

129. August, "Messianic Hope of Genesis," 46. August argues that—contra the higher critical notion that contends the New Testament authors imposed a foreign theology onto the Old Testament texts—". . . so long as the interpreter consistently applies the grammatical-historical method of interpretation, a thoroughly anticipatory view of the OT'S nature will emerge" (47). He successfully argues that the anticipatory view of the hope of the Messiah is the warp and woof that starts in Gen 3:15 and runs through the rest of Old Testament salvation history, being finally realized with the life, death, burial, and resurrection of Christ Jesus.

130. White, "Agony, Irony, and Victory," 172.

Inaugurated Eschatology and the Two-Ages Model

shed blood in Revelation 1:6.[131] White says, "That the victory of Christ took place at his death is clear from John's reference to his blood (1:6)." White says that "without at all denying the victory in Christ's resurrection, the irony of victory in Christ's death is palpable."[132]

Again, White points to another passage from Revelation 5:5–10. Here, he observes, is another exodus imagery of victory. In this passage the theme of victory is explicit. White sees that the lion imagery associated with the Davidic dynasty in verse 5 is applied to interpret Christ's qualification. As White says, John refers to David for two reasons: first, the Davidic king's mission was to wage holy war in order to secure God's people and make them pure for fellowship with God; second, he "places the holy war victory of this lion in the past by stating that he 'has overcome.'"[133] The point being this: Jesus, the lion, has already waged war against the malevolent forces of Satan that threatens the church.[134] This reality serves as the basis for repeated exhortations for the church to overcome in Revelation 2–3. The question before us is: when, where, and how did Christ (the lion) win victory over the forces of evil? The answer is in Revelation 5:6, 9:

> And between the throne and the four living creatures and among the elders I saw a Lamb standing, as though it had been slain, with seven horns and with seven eyes, which are the seven spirits of God sent out into all the earth. . . . And they sang a new song, saying, "Worthy are you to take the scroll and to open its seals, for you were slain, and by your blood you ransomed people for God from every tribe and language and people and nation.

Christ is not only depicted as a victorious lion, but in this passage Christ is also revealed as a slain Lamb standing, a slain Lamb standing that is characterized by having omnipotence ("seven horns") and omniscience ("seven eyes") and being full of the Spirit ("seven spirits"). As White astutely observes, this "slain lamb thus represents the image of a conqueror who was mortally wounded while defeating an enemy."[135] In short, Christ's death as the end-time messianic Lamb is interpreted as a sacrifice that ironically conquers. Beale says this:

131. White, "Agony, Irony, and Victory," 172.
132. White, "Agony, Irony, and Victory," 172.
133. White, "Agony, Irony, and Victory," 172.
134. Beale takes the verb ἐνίκησεν as a consummative aorist. Beale, *Book of Revelation*, 350
135. White, "Agony, Irony, and Victory," 173.

Kingdom Theology

> There is no doubt that v 6 portrays Jesus as resurrected and that the resurrection is crucial to his overcoming. He conquered death by being raised from the dead. But the present victorious effect of the Lamb's overcoming resides not only in the fact that the Lamb continues to "stand" but also in the fact that it continues to exist as a slaughtered Lamb. . . . In addition to the resurrection, the defeat of death was itself ironically a victory for Christ. That is, Christ as a Lion overcame by being slaughtered as a Lamb, which is the critical event in chapter 5. . . . Consequently, the Lion conquers initially by suffering as a slain lamb.[136]

Beale asks a key question:

> But how is the paradox of "conquering through suffering" to be understood more precisely?... Christ himself overcame by maintaining his loyalty to the Father through suffering and finally death (cf. 1:5). He was physically defeated but spiritually victorious. He willingly submitted to the unjust penalty of death, which was imposed on him ultimately by the devil. As an innocent victim he became a representative penal substitute for the sins of his people. While he was suffering the defeat of death, he was also overcoming by creating a kingdom of redeemed subjects over whom he would reign and over whom the devil would no longer have power . . . . Therefore, while Jesus was being defeated at the cross, he was nevertheless beginning to establish his kingdom. . . . This does not mean that the Lamb's resurrection is not conceived as a victory but only that there is an intention to highlight the death as a victory.[137]

It's clear here that we see the "irony of redemptive victory": though Satan and his seed intended to defeat him by means of the cross, the cross became the means by which Satan and his seed have been defeated. Christ's death was the means by which Satan and his seed intended to defeat him, but Christ's death ironically became the means by which he defeated Satan and his seed. God reversed Satan intention and established it as the means of victory.

This ironic pattern of redemptive victory becomes the pattern for the church's victory in history as depicted in the book of Revelation. White says that this is clear from the following considerations. First, in Revelation 1:5–6, 9, believers are identified with Christ's resurrection and kingship, making believers a kingdom. The question is: how does the church reign

---

136. Beale, *Book of Revelation*, 352–53.
137. Beale, *Book of Revelation*, 353–54.

INAUGURATED ESCHATOLOGY AND THE TWO-AGES MODEL

now as a kingdom? John is clear that he sees the saints victoriously reigning in history. In Revelation 1:9, John acknowledges the tension; that is, saints, while being members in the kingdom of God, also partner patiently while enduring tribulation. Patiently enduring tribulation is the present mode of victory and dominion in this present age. Beale makes this observation:

> The exercise of rule in this kingdom begins and continues only as one faithfully endures tribulation. This is a formula for kingship: faithful endurance through tribulation is the means by which one reigns in the present with Jesus. Believers are not mere subjects in Christ's kingdom. "Fellow partaker" underscores the active involvement of saints not only in enduring tribulation, but also in reigning in the midst of tribulation. Such kingship will be intensified at death (e.g., 2:10–11) and consummated at Jesus' final Parousia (cf. 21:1–22:5).[138]

Beale continues:

> This ironic exercise of rule is modeled on that of Christ, who revealed his veiled kingship on earth before his exaltation by enduring suffering and death in order to achieve his heavenly rule (cf. 1:5). Just as Christ ruled in a veiled way through suffering, so do Christians, which argues against the proposal that saints do not exercise kingship until the final coming of Christ when they are exalted over their enemies.[139]

Beale concludes that believers who overcome the world by patiently enduring tribulation without compromise ironically are overcome by the world too: "Hence, the church that perseveres in its witnessing faith wins a victory on earth even though it suffers earthly defeat."[140] In short, this is how we are to understand God's victorious reign and dominion within history. This is how we understand God's reign in this age in Christ Jesus and his church in spite of cultural dissonance and declension. In short, in spite of the cultural dissonance and declension, the inauguration of the kingdom of God's new creation is a present reality and the consummation of the kingdom of God's new creation is an inevitable reality!

---

138. Beale, *Book of Revelation*, 201.
139. Beale, *Book of Revelation*, 201–2.
140. Beale, *Book of Revelation*, 269.

CHAPTER 3

PRACTICAL IMPLICATIONS
Mission of the Church

NOW THAT WE HAVE a working definition and understanding of the kingdom of God's inaugurated new creation as the new-creational reign of God, and, second, a working understanding of God's victorious reign within history, including God's victorious reign within history through his church, these understandings can serve as a theological foundation and model of orientation for ministry. This inaugurated notion of the kingdom of God not only forms and informs the structure of New Testament eschatology, according to Vos, but also practical issues regarding the church's notion of ministry. How one understands the concept of the kingdom of God's inaugurated new creation has many practical implications for ministry. In this chapter, I will be addressing the practical implications of the inaugurated kingdom of God's new creation regarding the mission of the church. My thesis is that since the inauguration of the kingdom of God's new creation is an "already" current reality in this present age, and the consummation of the kingdom of God's new creation is a "not yet" future inevitability for the age to come—both being the work of God and God alone, which has been demonstrated above—and if the message (that is, the gospel) of the inauguration of the kingdom of God's new creation is something God's people are mandated to witness, proclaim, and pronounce to the world (as will be demonstrated), then the mission of God's people is very narrow and specific, which will also be demonstrated below. Mission creep is a real concern for the contemporary church. Navigating the missional landscape without losing our purpose is a must. Below, I will posit two models for

PRACTICAL IMPLICATIONS

mission—that is, the holistic and the missional models—which lend themselves to mission creep.

MODELS FOR MISSIONS

Köstenberger is correct when he notes that

> A church that is unsure of its mission will not be effective in carrying it out.... The church cannot afford to let urgent needs or pressing circumstances set its agenda. That agenda has already been set in its parameters by Jesus and needs to be defined and understood in relation to Jesus' mission.[1]

If urgent needs and circumstances cannot define the church's agenda for mission, then what should define the church's agenda for mission? The church's mission must be circumscribed and defined and understood in relation to king Jesus' mission and mandate. King Jesus' model and mandate for missions should be our starting point. Even though the church's mission is not identical to Christ's earthly mission—that is, Christ completed his mission in toto without failure, and his mission was unique to his person (incarnation) and work (atonement)—nonetheless King Jesus is continuing to communicate through us what he has inaugurated (for example, see Acts 1:1). What is Christ Jesus continuing to communicate through his church in light of his inauguration of the kingdom of God's new creation? The answer is missions. The question then is: how do we understand mission(s) in light of said inaugurated eschatology?

The Holistic Model

There are a number of theological approaches[2] that can serve as a model for the church's mission. One such approach has been called the "incarnational model," displayed in Jesus' ministry. According to Köstenberger, the

---

1. Köstenberger, *Mission of Jesus*, 219.

2. I will forego approaches that are not evangelical, namely liberationist theological approaches and social gospel approaches within the larger Protestant liberal tradition.

most "pronounced advocate"³ of this approach is John Stott.⁴ John Stott contends that both evangelism and social action are constitutive of a full-orbed notion of missions. As Stott says, "We are sent into the world, like Jesus, to serve."⁵ We serve in two distinct ways: the biblical synthesis of evangelism and social responsibility.⁶

Stott considers his approach to missions to be a mediating position between two extremes.⁷ On the one hand, there is the extreme of the "older or traditional view," and, on the other hand, there is the extreme of the "ecumenical" view. Regarding the former, Stott says that mission entails "verbal proclamation."⁸ The image is that of a "preacher," paternalistically reaching the lost. The only "real mission" that counts is evangelistic preaching, not "schools and hospitals."⁹ This traditional view, says Stott, doesn't outright eschew education and medical work, but said work is viewed as a "useful adjunct to evangelical work" or a step toward the real work of evangelism, "providing their patients and pupils a conveniently captive audience for the gospel."¹⁰

---

3. An example of this can be seen in John Stott and Christopher J. H. Wright, *Christian Mission in the Modern World: What The Church Should Be Doing Now*, Updated and Expanded, (Downers Grove, IL: InterVarsity, 2015), 24–25. Stott argues that there are two aspects of the mission of Jesus that are paralleled in the mission of the church. The first is the relationship between evangelism and social action; the second is "the principle of incarnation." What he means by the incarnational principle is that instead of "shouting the gospel at people from a distance" to unbelievers, believers should be involved "deeply in their lives, to think ourselves into their culture and problems." Köstenberger makes too much of this. Stott is explicit that Jesus' incarnation is unique, that the church can never engage incarnationally as our Lord. Stott spills very little ink on the "incarnational approach" to missions. Stott means only that the church must engage people at their level, not to pontificate as a distance on high. Michael Horton superbly critiques those who have pressed the incarnational approach too far, calling it a "kenotic path" that empties the Great Commission of its "divinely authorized methods." See Michael Horton, *The Gospel Commission: Recovering God's Strategy For Making Disciples*, (Grand Rapids: Baker Books, 2011), 117–132.

4. Köstenberger, *Mission of Jesus*, 213.

5 Stott and Wright, *Christian Mission*, 24.

6. Stott and Wright, *Christian Mission*, 20.

7. Stott and Wright, *Christian Mission*, 16.

8. Stott and Wright, *Christian Mission*, 16.

9. Stott and Wright, *Christian Mission*, 16.

10. Stott and Wright, *Christian Mission*, 17.

Practical Implications

The Traditional View

What is the "traditional view"? Stott observes that the traditional view dovetails well with a pessimistic view of culture and society at large; that society is doomed and will be destroyed, that the "Christian's only duty is to mount a rescue operation," that any attempt to "improve society" is a fool's errand. It's a fool's errand because "Jesus is coming at any moment"; there is no time to "build a new world." "It is too late" to spiritually recruit enough born-again people to make a difference so that "society [might] conceivably be reborn." To be fair, Stott does not say that such a negative eschatological notion of this age[11] is causally related, just that there is "sometimes" a correlation between societal dystopia and the traditional view of missions.

Though Stott does not develop or elaborate on how one's reading of eschatology causally influences one's notion of missions, it strongly suggests that Stott does in fact believe that eschatology does form and inform one's notion of missions. Stott is clear that biblical revelation should shape the church's notion of the image of God as Creator. It's the image of God as Creator who "gave humanity a 'cultural mandate' to subdue and rule the earth, who instituted governing authorities as his 'ministers' to order society and maintain justice."[12] It's Stott's contention that the traditional view, formed and informed by a negative eschatological notion of this age, is "only partially shaped by biblical revelation" because it rejects the original "cultural mandate" given by God as Creator.[13] Suffice it to say, Stott sees that both protology (namely the cultural mandate), and eschatology have very practical implications concerning one's notion of missions.

The Ecumenical View

On the other hand, Stott contends that there is the other extreme that is equally unbiblical vis-à-vis the traditional view; that is, the "ecumenical view." The ecumenical view seeks to establish *shalom*, which he calls "social harmony." Such attempts at social harmony are deemed to be the very work of God, that is, the *Missio Dei*. God's mission is immanent, working in and

---

11. Stott does not elaborate on what particular notion of eschatology characterizes such a pessimistic view.

12. Stott and Wright, *Christian Mission*, 16. Here Stott is citing the Lausanne Covenant, paragraph 5. See it at https://lausanne.org/content/covenant/Lausanne-covenant#cov.

13. Stott and Wright, *Christian Mission*, 16.

through historical processes. Such historical processes are "identical with the kingdom of God," conflating the two into one.[14] The kingdom of God is reified and typified in such things ". . . as the battle against racism, the humanization of industrial relations, the overcoming of class divisions, community development, and the quest for an ethic of honesty and integrity in business and other professions," just to name a few.[15] As Stott correctly points out, the ecumenical view has the world setting the agenda for the church regarding missions because God's primary relationship is no longer with the church but to the world. The formula is no longer "God-church-world." It's "God-world-church."[16]

In short, it's the "contemporary sociological needs" of the world and its concomitant social renewal that sets the missional agenda of the church. Stott offers four robust critiques of the ecumenical view, but suffice it to say he perceptively observes that missions cannot denote everything God is doing in the world. He says, "In providence and common grace he is indeed active in all people and all societies, whether they acknowledge him or not. But this is not his 'mission.' 'Mission' concerns his redeemed people, and what he sends them into the world to do."[17]

The Via Media

In light of these two diametrically opposed extremes, Stott proffers a middle way, a "better way."[18] This middle way arises out of the nature of God, not the nature of the church. The nature of God is revealed in the Bible, and it's the God of revelation that reveals himself as a "sending God."[19] As Stott says, "God is love, always reaching out after others in self-giving service." Stott gives a number of examples, such as Abraham being sent forth, "commanding him to go from his country and kindred . . . promising to bless him and to bless the world through him if he obeyed (Genesis 12:1–13)." Another is Joseph, whom God sent to Egypt ". . . to preserve a godly remnant on earth during the famine (Genesis 45:4–8)." God also sent Moses ". . . with the good news of liberation, saying to him, 'Come, I will send you

---

14. Stott and Wright, *Christian Mission*, 18.
15. Stott and Wright, *Christian Mission*, 18.
16. Stott and Wright, *Christian Mission*, 18.
17. Stott and Wright, *Christian Mission*, 19.
18. Stott and Wright, *Christian Mission*, 20.
19. Stott and Wright, *Christian Mission*, 21.

Practical Implications

to Pharaoh that you may bring forth my people . . . out of Egypt' (Exodus 3:10)." Stott's point is that "throughout the history of Israel God sent all of his prophets that His people may repent and turn from their wicked ways, but they would not listen per Jeremiah 7:25, 26." Then Stott points to God sending the last and final prophet, God's own Son, in the person and work of the Spirit on the day of Pentecost; these are just a few examples Stott points to that demonstrate the nature of God being a "sending God."[20] This, he says, is the "essential biblical background" to understand mission, especially the "primal mission" of God sending "his prophets, his Son, his Spirit." Of these three missions, Stott observes, it's the sending of his son that is the epicenter of missions. It's the Son who sends as he was sent.

This brings Stott to the consideration of the Great Commission. Stott concedes that most versions of the Lord's commission given—namely Matthew 28:16–20, Luke 24:44-49; Mark 16:15 (including the redaction of Mark that expresses the missionary impulse of the early church, which added the longer ending in Mark); and Acts 1:8—emphasize evangelism. He says that the "cumulative emphases seems clear: it is placed on preaching, witnessing, and making disciples . . . [making] the mission of the church according to the specification of the risen Lord . . . exclusively a preaching, converting, and teaching mission."[21] Stott also confesses that at one time he had argued from the traditional perspective before the World Congress on Evangelism in Berlin in 1966.[22] Before, Stott used to believe that social responsibility was an implication of the Great Commission, that social responsibility is one among many repercussions. But he now believes that he was mistaken, that he sees "more clearly" that social responsibility is not only a consequence of the Great Commission, but it's "the actual Commission itself"; that both evangelism and social responsibility are constitutive of the Great Commission.[23] Stott comes to this conclusion through his study of the Johannine form of the Great Commission. Stott points to what he sees as a sort of proleptic version of the Great Commission in John 17:18, where Jesus says, "As you sent me into the world, so I have sent them into the world." Stott says that Jesus took this prayer statement in the upper room and turned it into a formal commission in John 20:21: "Jesus said to them again, 'Peace be with you. As the Father has sent me, even so I am

---

20. Stott and Wright, *Christian Mission*, 21.
21. Stott and Wright, *Christian Mission*, 22.
22. Stott and Wright, *Christian Mission*, 22.
23. Stott and Wright, *Christian Mission*, 23.

Kingdom Theology

sending you.'" From this Stott argues that Jesus' mission is the "model of ours."

In what way does Stott understand that the pattern and purpose of Jesus' mission is our mission, that Jesus' mandate is our mandate? Stott acknowledges that Jesus' incarnation is unique, that Jesus as the eternal, pre-incarnate Son was sent by the Father into the world (God enfleshed) to be the Savior of the world, that is, "to atone for our sins and to bring eternal life (1 John 4:9, 10, 14)."[24] Christ's person and work (the incarnation and atonement) were both his "major purpose" and "unique." Yet, Stott says that "all this is still an inadequate statement of why he came."[25] Curiously, Stott says it's inadequate because Christ's person and work are too specific. This is implied by Stott preferring the "general" notion of serving over the particular notion of the person and work of Christ. Just as "The Son of man . . . came not to be served but to serve, and to give his life as a ransom for many" (Mark 10:45), likewise "he sends us. . . . Therefore, our mission, like his, is to be one of service."[26]

In what form should that service come? Stott contends that it should come in the form of a "servant role," a servant role that combines "evangelism and social action." Just as for Christ, it should be for us that both evangelism and social action should assist as "authentic expressions of the love that serves,"[27] serves both spiritual (evangelism) and physical (social action) needs. Stott calls this "our total Christian responsibility." In short, social action is as much a mandate as evangelism.

Before Stott justifies his assertion, he first defines the relationship between evangelism and social action. He notes that there have been three approaches. First, there is the approach that regards "social action as a means to evangelism."[28] Stott says having an ulterior motive "breeds so-called rice Christians." He calls this a "cloak of humanitarian work." Quoting Gandhi, ". . . why should I change my religion because a doctor who professes Christianity as his religion has cured me from some disease?"[29] Second, Stott says, there is a sacramental approach. This position is an improvement, in that instead of social actions being a means to evangelism, it is a

---

24. Stott and Wright, *Christian Mission*, 23.
25. Stott and Wright, *Christian Mission*, 23.
26. Stott and Wright, *Christian Mission*, 24.
27. Stott and Wright, *Christian Mission*, 24.
28. Stott and Wright, *Christian Mission*, 25.
29. Stott and Wright, *Christian Mission*, 26.

"manifestation of evangelism." Social action is not an arbitrary attachment but "grows out of it as a natural expression."[30] Stott goes so far as to say that social action is the "sacrament of evangelism," by making the message visible. Stott says that we see this sacramental nature in the words and actions of Jesus: "His words and deeds belong together; the words interpret the deeds, and the deeds embody the words." As noted, this is an improvement for Stott; however, he is still "uneasy" with this approach. The reason is because social action is a subset of evangelism.[31] The third way is Stott's preferred way: "social action is a partner of evangelism."[32] Stott says that evangelism is independent of social action, and vice versa. Social action "stands on its own feet in its own right alongside the other."[33]

To justify his assertion, Stott points to 1 John 3:17–18: "But if anyone has the world's goods and sees his brother in need, yet closes his heart against him, how does God's love abide in him? Little children, let us not love in word or talk but in deed and in truth." Stott gleans from John a twofold condition: "first, 'seeing' a brother in need and second 'having' the wherewithal to meet the need."[34] This is what Stott calls the principle of "love in action." This principle applies to the "nature of the seen need." If I see a spiritual need, then the gospel meets the need. If I see a physical need, then social action and its resources—that is, medical, educational, social expertise, etc.—will meet that need. Stott concedes that there is a "diversity of Christian callings," and said action, be it evangelical or social, and these callings should comport with one's calling. He says, "The doctor must not neglect the practice of medicine for evangelism, and neither should the evangelist be distracted from the ministry of the word by the ministry of tables, as the apostles quickly discovered (Acts 6.)"[35]

For the sake of argument, Stott says, "But suppose someone remains convinced that the Great Commission relates exclusively to evangelism, what then?" Jesus did not leave us with only one set of instructions. Stott observes, Jesus also left us with the "second and great commandment," that is, to love our neighbor as ourselves. This means we are ". . . to give ourselves actively and constructively to serve our neighbor's welfare." In the final

30. Stott and Wright, *Christian Mission*, 24.
31. Stott and Wright, *Christian Mission*, 24.
32. Stott and Wright, *Christian Mission*, 27.
33. Stott and Wright, *Christian Mission*, 27.
34. Stott and Wright, *Christian Mission*, 27.
35. Stott and Wright, *Christian Mission*, 28.

analysis, our Lord left us with two mandates: both the Great Commission and the Great Commandment.[36]

In a later work, Stott elaborates on the biblical justification for the partnership of evangelism and social action in light of said two mandates.[37] He first points to the character of God as both Creator and Redeemer who cares for the "total well-being (spiritual and material) of all the human beings he has made."[38] Based on this distinction, on the one hand, God "yearns after his creatures in their lostness." In this yearning God offers salvation through the person and work of Christ. However, on the other hand, God cares not only for the spiritual needs but for the material needs of the poor, the hungry, the alien, the widow and the orphan. Stott contends that the mandate of the Great Commission attends the former, while the mandate of the Great Commandment attends the latter. Both mandates reflect the character of God, eschewing the notion of "dualism in the thinking of God."[39]

Second, not only is the partnership of the two mandates grounded in the character of God, but it is also grounded in the ministry and teaching of Jesus. Stott notes that Jesus' ministry was a ministry that announced the kingdom of God. He correctly notes that, on the one hand, Jesus announced the kingdom by preaching the message of the kingdom, that is, the gospel message of salvation, and, on the other hand, Jesus demonstrated the arrival of the kingdom by "works of compassion and power." Stott quotes Mark 6:6 and Acts 10:38, where Jesus went about doing both: teaching and "doing good and healing."[40] Stott sees in the ministry of Jesus "an indissoluble bond between evangelism and compassion ministry," an inviolable bond between both mandates: the Great Commission and the Great Commandment.[41] As Chuck Colson notes, "He was concerned not only with saving man from hell in the next world, but with delivering him from the hellishness of this one."[42] In this context, Stott says,

> ... words remain abstract until they are made concrete in deeds of love, while works remain ambiguous until they are interpreted by

---

36. Stott and Wright, *Christian Mission*, 29.
37. Stott, *Contemporary Church*.
38. Stott, *Contemporary Church*, 343.
39. Stott, *Contemporary Church*, 344.
40. Stott, *Contemporary Church*, 345.
41. Stott, *Contemporary Church*, 345.
42. Colson, *Loving God*, 145.

the proclamation of the gospel. Words without works lack credibility; works without words lack clarity. So Jesus' works made his words visible; his words made his works intelligible.[43]

The third and final argument for the partnership of both evangelism and social action is that both mandates are grounded in the nature of the communication of the gospel. Stott contends that just as the gospel communicates to human beings in both verbal form and by means of Christ's incarnation, that is, the Word become flesh, likewise our words must communicate God's love with action; social actions visibly demonstrate God's love.

CRITIQUE OF THE HOLISTIC MODEL

In short, Stott offers a holistic model or approach to missions. Before I move on to the second model of missions, let me offer a critique of Stott's holistic approach. First, Stott asserts that "missions" is constitutive of both evangelism as well as social action (that is, love of neighbor). These are distinct without mixture or confusion, separation or division. Stott likens these two parts of missions as two rivers diverging from a single mandate of the Great Commission. However, he has not shown by Scripture or argument, but has merely asserted that the mandate of the Great Commission is the fountainhead of both evangelism and social action. But how can the Great Commission be the mandate for social action if social action—that is, love of neighbor—is something commanded of all people, and active in all people from one degree to another, not just Christians? Again he says, "In providence and common grace [God] is indeed active in all people and all societies, whether they acknowledge him or not. But this is not his 'mission.' 'Mission" concerns his redeemed people, and what he sends them into the world to do." Here he undercuts his argument that the Great Commission is the fountainhead of social action, because the mission of the church is something only the redeemed are sent into the world to do, and only the redeemed can do. Stott correctly contends that evangelism is the exclusive domain of the church, that evangelism is the unique priority that only the church is mandated to do.[44] Social action is the consequence and/or product of providence and common grace. So how can Stott say that

---

43. Stott, *Contemporary Church*, 345.
44. Colson, *Loving God*, 58–59.

Kingdom Theology

the Great Commission is the fountainhead of social action if social action is not unique to the mission of the church?

Stott does have a good point that, unlike the Great Commission texts in the Synoptic Gospels, the accent in the Gospel of John regarding the Great Commission is the Christian's role of servanthood: just as Jesus came to serve, the Christian is to serve. However, he states that service as evangelism or service as social action (as stated above) "comports with one's calling." Again Stott says, "The doctor must not neglect the practice of medicine for evangelism, and neither should the evangelist be distracted from the ministry of the word by the ministry of tables, as the apostles quickly discovered (Acts 6)."[45] Stott makes a very important distinction, an essential distinction: that is, a Christian's vocation vs. the church's vocation. But suffice it to say, when an evangelist evangelizes or the pastor preaches the gospel, that is the work of the Lord, a work unique to the church as church. However, when a physician attends to what ails his patient, that is not the work of the Lord unique to the church as church. Again with this second quote from Stott, he seriously and acutely undercuts his argument once again that the Great Commission is the fountainhead of both evangelism and social action.

Second, because of the perceived weakness of his argument, Stott pivots from saying the Great Commission is the fountainhead of both evangelism and social action, to now saying that even if (for the sake of argument) it is not justifiable to say that the mandate of the Great Commission is constitutive of both evangelism and social action, to now saying the Great Commission is not the only mandate given to the church; there is a second mandate: that is, the Great Commandment to love one's neighbor. Both the mandate to evangelize and the mandate to social action are unavoidable; they are both binding on all Christians, says Stott. This argument on the surface is much stronger. Who can deny that there are two great mandates: the Great Commission and the Great Commandment? It's patently true and clearly taught in Scripture that the second table of the law is a mandate to love our neighbor. The Westminster Standards are clear that the second table of the law does entail social action, social benevolence, and acts of mercy to all of mankind—that is, love of our neighbor's welfare. However, even on this point Stott undercuts his argument. Stott is very sensitive to the accusation

---

45. Colson, *Loving God*, 28.

that the holistic approach to mission is actually the old "social gospel" in the vein of Rauschenbusch.[46] He denies this objection by saying,

> ... isn't this going back to the old "social gospel?" No, it is not. We must distinguish between the social gospel of the theological liberalism, developed by Walter Rauschenbusch and his friends at the beginning of this century, and the social implications of the biblical gospel.[47]

I agree with Stott that his approach is not the old social gospel, but again he seems to undercut his argument. He said earlier that social action is not an implication of missions (that is, evangelism), but stands on its own, that social responsibility is in fact not a consequence or implication of missions. But here he says social action is in fact an implication of the gospel.

To summarize Stott's holistic approach, Stott has not convincingly demonstrated that social action is either constitutive of the singular mandate of the Great Commission or the fruit of the Great Commandment. The moral obligation of the Great Commandment is not unique to individual Christians, but is universalizable to man in general; it's the moral law within, republished in the giving of the Decalogue, yet a mandate and obligation written on the hearts of all men.[48]

---

46. Stott, *Contemporary Church*, 350.

47. Stott, *Contemporary Church*, 350.

48. The question must be asked: even though unregenerate man is obliged to love one's neighbor, to walk according to the mandate of the Great Commandment written on the heart of all men, can man in fact live up to said commandment? This is where making a distinction of covenants and the three uses of the moral law is helpful regarding moral agency. Under the covenant of works and in light of the first and theological use of the law, mankind (including both the regenerate and unregenerate) is incapable of loving his or her neighbor (Second Great Commandment) much less God (First Great Commandment). At most, all the law can do as intended is to bring conviction and condemnation to the heart of man. Under the covenant of grace and in light of the third use of the law, only the regenerate is capable of loving one's neighbor with true charity (though very imperfectly because of a mixture of motives and intentions) because the standard of said subjective, moral righteousness (in contrast to objective, legal righteousness), is based on the motive and intent of one's heart to glorify God. In this context, the law provides moral guidance according to Calvin. (As I will share below, God in Christ has restored said glory in man through Christ, making it possible for regenerate man to glorify God in his actions and motives and intent as the law functions as a road map of holiness.) However, under the covenant of common grace and in light of the second and civil use of the law, the unregenerate is capable of loving his or her neighbor neither in the light of true charity nor in the light of bringing glory to God, but for the preservation of man, the preservation of social order, and the preservation and promotion of the common good, which redounds to the advantage of the unregenerate—all in order to restrain

Kingdom Theology

The Missional Model

This takes me to a second possible alternative: that is, the missional model. The missional model (as with the holistic) is also broader than the traditionally limited notion of those actions and ministries taken on by the church to present, witness, and proclaims the gospel to the unregenerate. Michael Williams argues that it's more than evangelism, because God is doing more than evangelism. And since God is doing more than evangelism, it follows (Williams contends) that his people are called to do more, that is, called to a broader range of cultural engagement in the world in which we live.

Williams argues that Christian mission is a missional collaboration with the *Missio Dei*.[49] In fact, "God's goal is that his people will join in the divine redemptive action toward the world."[50] As Williams says:

> Scripture is not simply a cognitive deposit of propositions, but actually a call to join in the divine action; we must read the text with that action in mind, looking for it, and asking how we are being shaped and enlisted to participate in the action. Thus, the "so what" or the "what then" question is just as important as the

---

evil. Jesus in Matt 7:11 says, "If you then, who are evil, know how to give good gifts to your children, how much more will your Father who is in heaven give good things to those who ask him!" In what context is Jesus speaking of good gifts? Are the good gifts of physical and emotional love, support, and care (Second Great Commandment) under the covenant of works? No, earthly fathers are evil. What about under the covenant of grace? No, some evil fathers are unregenerate (granted that evil fathers here includes not only unregenerate men but regenerate men who are evil compared to God the Father). Then Christ must be speaking of under the covenant of common grace. Unregenerate (evil) fathers can and do "know how to give good gifts" even if the motive is not true virtue. Calvin calls this a "mercenary love" because it's in regard to one's advantage. The civil use of the law (moral restraint and preservation) under the administration of the covenant of common grace is the best that the unregenerate man (evil father) can do in a fallen world. This is evident in that even though the image of God in man as a rational, moral agent is not annihilated, it is radically deformed, defaced, and disfigured. The bare virtue of the "virtuous pagan" is still vice.

49. Bosch, *Transforming Mission*, 389. Bosch defines the Missio Dei as "God's self-revelation as the One who loves the world, God's involvement in and with the world, the nature and activity of God, which embraces both the church and the world, and in which the church is privileged to participate. Missio Dei enunciates the good news that God is a God-for-people." Bosch correctly notes that the mission of God is first not the activity of the church in the world, but first the activity of God in the world as the church participates with God. The primary agent is God, not the church.

50. Williams, "Theology as Witness," 74.

"what is it" biblical content question of classical evangelical and Reformed Christianity.[51]

I agree with the notion that the "what then" question of implication is as important as the "what is it" question of theology or content, hence the structure of my project. However, is the *Missio Dei*, that is, mission of God, coterminous with the mission of the church? Christopher Wright is a distinguished proponent of what some call the "missional" approach.[52] Wright contends that the "controlling theme" of all of Scripture is missions.[53] He says, "Mission is a major key that unlocks the whole grand narrative of the canon of Scripture."[54] Contrary to Beale (who argues that new-creational kingdom is the center), Wright contends that mission is the center of the redemptive-historical progressive unfolding of God's ultimate plan of the "new-creational kingdom." Mission is the controlling theme of Scripture, where both God and man collaborate in the redemptive-historical progressive unfolding of God's plan, where the mission of God is coterminous with the mission of the church. This is why Wright contends that mission is "a major key that unlocks the whole grand narrative of the canon of Scripture."[55] Wright calls Scripture "the story of God's mission through God's people in their engagement with God's world for the redemption of God's creation."[56]

In light of this, how does Wright define mission? Wright offers a definition that sounds traditional: mission is "our committed participation as God's people, at God's invitation and command, in God's own mission within the history of God's world for the redemption of God's creation."[57] In a later work (contrary to the maxim, "If everything is mission, then nothing is mission"), he says, "If everything is mission . . . everything is mission." And if everything is mission, then the traditional, limited notion of mission as being "cross-cultural evangelistic mission"[58] can't delimit mis-

---

51. Williams, "Theology as Witness," 75.

52. McNeal, *Missional Renaissance*, 29. McNeal defines the missional church as "the people of God partnering with God in his redemptive mission in the world," which is constitutive of every good thing a Christian can do.

53. C. J. H. Wright, *Mission of God's People*, 26.

54. C. J. H. Wright, *Mission of God*, 17.

55. C. J. H. Wright, *Mission of God*, 17.

56. C. J. H. Wright, *Mission of God*, 23.

57. C. J. H. Wright, *Mission of God*, 23.

58. C. J. H. Wright, *Mission of God's People*, 26.

Kingdom Theology

sion because cross-cultural, evangelistic mission, in particular, and those actions and ministries taken on by the local church to present, witness, and proclaim the gospel to the unregenerate, in general, do not circumscribe everything that God is doing in the world. Wright says, ". . . everything a Christian [that is, individual Christian vocation] and a Christian church [that is, the institutional church or corporate, visible body of Christ] is, says, and does should be missional in its conscious participation in the mission of God in God's world."[59] It seems for Wright, that the notion of "conscious participation" or "committed participation" functions as a synonym for "missional." "Missional" as it's used in many quarters is much broader than "mission." As DeYoung and Gilbert note, "It's a big trunk that can smuggle a great deal of unwanted baggage."[60] Why is missional thinking broader than missions? In part for Wright, it is because the traditional, narrower, and limited notion of missions—that is, limited to those actions and ministries taken on by the church to present, witness, and proclaim the gospel to the unregenerate—is based on a "damaging false dichotomy."[61] This false dichotomy is based on the distinction between the sacred realm vs. the secular realm, with missions being subsumed under the sphere of the sacred and not the secular. Wright says the result is that

> . . . mission is something either that specifically commissioned Christians manage to do full-time, if they can get enough "support" to do so, or something that other Christians (the vast majority) do in odd moments of time they have to spare from the necessity of having to work for a living. Maybe they can fit "a mission trip" into a vacation, or go on a "church mission" over the weekend.[62]

In short, missions according to the missional approach must include the sacred as well as the secular. The missional is all of life with no "damaging false dichotomy." An example of Wright's notion of conscious participation—aka missional activities in all of life, not delimited by such a false dichotomy—includes things like the public arenas of business, education, politics, medicine, sports, etc.[63] Wright rhetorically asks, "Is it only the moments of evangelistic opportunities in the world, or can our work itself

---

59. C. J. H. Wright, *Mission of God's People*, 26.

60. DeYoung and Gilbert, *What Is the Mission*, 21. Both men have concerns about missional thinking.

61. C. J. H. Wright, *Mission of God's People*, 27.

62. C. J. H. Wright, *Mission of God's People*, 27–28.

63. C. J. H. Wright, *Mission of God's People*, 28.

participate in God's mission?" His answer is, yes! Yes, both types of works participate in God's mission. The conversion of a sinner being forgiven and justified by faith by means of evangelism is no more redemptive than Christians seeking to be good ecological stewards of the planet by means of Christian vocation. Wright maintains that missions cannot be reduced to the Great Commission, that missions is more than evangelism and Christian edification.[64] The scope and extent of God's mission in redemption through Christ to all creation is also the people of God's mission. Wright says,

> Clearly, a fully biblical theology and practice of mission must take account of a fully biblical account of sin. Mission strategies that focus exclusively on individual human wrongdoing and applying the remedy of the gospel solely in that realm cannot, of course, be blamed for lack of biblical zeal in that one evangelistic field. However, they do fall short of a full biblical understanding of all that sin is and does, and inevitably fall short likewise of a full understanding of all that the gospel addresses and all that our mission must engage.[65]

Wright is explicit that the mission of the church is identical to the mission of God, that the scope of the mission of God is one and the same as the scope of the mission of God's people. Just as the mission of God is not reduced to evangelism or the Great Commission, likewise the mission of God's people cannot be reduced to the Great Commission.

In conclusion, what place then does the Great Commission take within the missional schema? Some in the Reformed tradition argue that the Great Commission should not be given primacy. Williams says,

> Some folks in the Reformed camp who have championed the doctrine of creation and a restorational eschatology over the years have been tempted to say that evangelism is no more important than relief missions, mercy ministries, Christian political action, and environmental concern. Christians are called to be redemptive agents in all spheres of life. As sin touches everything, from the biosphere to human social interactions and political-economic structures, the people of God are called to engage them all. Evangelism, proclaiming the good news, is for the whole of creation. It

---

64. C. J. H. Wright, *Mission of God*, 416.
65. C. J. H. Wright, *Mission of God*, 433.

is not just about getting people saved. And each redemptive action or ministry is as essential as any other.⁶⁶

Wright seems to agree with this line of thinking. For Wright the Great Commission has a place of priority, but it's a bare logical/chronological priority in the sense that before there is an order of Christian social action, there must first be Christians who have been evangelized and edified by the ordinary means of grace.⁶⁷ In the final analysis, both the mandate of Great Commission and the mandate the Great Commandment are equally redemptive, having equal preeminence.

CRITIQUE OF THE MISSIONAL MODEL

Before I move on, let me offer a summary critique. First, the missional model displaces the primacy of the Great Commission, relegating it to a logical/chronological place of priority, which is no primacy at all. This marginalizes the mandate of the Great Commission. This is one of my critiques of the missional approach. As I will argue below, Scripture is clear that not only does the mandate of the Great Commission take precedent over everything the church may do, but the mandate of the Great Commission is exactly that; that is, a mandate. Whatever else the institutional church may do in addition to the Great Commission (as for example, social action) is tangential. The raison d'etre of the church is the mandate of the Great Commission. When other foci come to the center, then the church loses focus, opening the door to mission creep.

Second is the missional center; Wright contends that missions is the center of the redemptive-historical progressive unfolding of God's ultimate plan of redemption, which includes the kingdom of God/new creation, that is, Beale's notion of new-creational kingdom, and among other biblical/theological thematic doctrines: for example, Christology, justification, sanctification, Pneumatology, etc. But this seems to be placing undue primacy upon the means rather than the ends. Missions is not an end to itself. Missions is a means to a greater end, which is the church's witness, proclamation, and pronouncement of the inauguration of the new-creational kingdom and its consummation. If missions is a means to a greater purpose, then I do not see how missions can serve as the hermeneutical center. It

---

66. Williams, *Theology as Witness*, 80.
67. C. J. H. Wright, *Mission of God*, 26.

seems more logical to posit that the kingdom of God's new creation is the purpose for the mission of God, as well as the mission of God's people.

Third, the missional approach wrongly assumes that the scope and extent and magnitude of the mission of God's church are coterminous with the mission of God. Just as the church is one limited aspect of the kingdom of God's new creation, namely, the visible outpost of the kingdom on earth, likewise the kingdom mission of God's people is one limited aspect of the mission of God's kingdom. For instance, the mission of God's kingdom, that is, the *Missio Dei*, is what God has accomplished and will accomplish in salvation history. God through Christ's vicarious atonement and resurrection accomplished salvation; that is, redemption is freedom from the penalty of sin through Christ's inauguration of the kingdom. God through Christ will accomplish salvation through Christ's consummation of the kingdom. This is the mission of God, but it's a mission in which the people of God (the institutional/visible church and individual Christian vocation in light of cultural engagement) do not partner with God. The people of God do not partner with God in accomplishing justification. Regeneration and justification and definitive and progressive sanctification, etc., are monergistic. Why would we think that the mission of God regarding ultimate shalom and cosmic regeneration and resurrection is any different? Since the inauguration of the kingdom of God's new creation and the consummation of the kingdom of God's new creation are not works that the mission of God's people collaborate on with God (which has been demonstrated), and if the kingdom of God is something the mission of God's people are to witness, proclaim, and pronounce to the world, then the mission of God's people is very narrow and specific. If the message (that is, the gospel) of the inauguration of the kingdom of God's new creation is one whereby the church is to proclaim, then the implication for the mission of the church is narrow and limited.

The Mission of the Church

This takes me to the traditional view, that is, a view more faithful to Scripture, a view that narrows the mission of the church. Before I move forward, I want to emphasize a point of agreement. If you recall, Stott asserts that there is a certain "pessimistic view" of culture and society that dovetails with the traditional view of mission. To be fair, Stott does not say that a pessimistic vision is the cause of the traditional view, but that there is a correlation.

Kingdom Theology

This pessimistic view is formed and informed by an eschatological vision that sees this age as doomed, irredeemable, and irretrievable, that sees that this world cannot be preserved from destruction, much less repaired or restored. What is the reason? There is not enough time for the Christian to devise a plan or implement a rescue mission to regenerate enough souls to redeem society. There is no more time left to preserve society, or regenerate society, or improve society, to "build a new world because Jesus is coming at any moment." If we had enough time to recruit an ample number of regenerate souls to make a difference, then "society [might] conceivably be reborn."[68] In part, the doctrine of the imminent return of Christ (that is, Christ can come at any moment) makes it not possible.

As noted earlier, Stott does in fact imply that one's notion of eschatology has real-life and practical implications for the church's mission, and not only for eschatology but also for protology. The image of God as Creator—that is, the Creator who gave humanity a "cultural mandate" to subdue and rule the earth, who instituted governing authorities as his "ministers" to order society and maintain justice, along with ordinary Christian men and women living out their various vocations—is an image of a God that can change the world through us! The reason why (as Stott contends) the traditional view separates social action from evangelism is because of its pessimistic lineaments, features, and contours concerning both eschatology (missions) and protology (creational/cultural mandate).

On this point, I agree wholeheartedly with Stott's criticism of some within the traditional camp. Some have taken a pessimistic "Christ against culture" approach to engaging culture due to particular notions of protology according to H. Richard Niebuhr.[69] Others have taken a pessimistic

---

68. See Hunter, *To Change the World*. Hunter calls this bottom up approach to understanding, engaging, and transforming culture the "common view," a view that he argues is based on a faulty "social imaginary."

69. Niebuhr, *Christ and Culture*, 45. Niebuhr contends that this particular pattern of cultural engagement is "both logically and chronologically primary" due to both the doctrine of the Lordship of Jesus in Scripture and Christian living in the apostolic age. In other words, the historical trajectory of moral and ontological dualism is the logical outcome of the Lordship of Christ instantiated in the lived experience of primitive church. Niebuhr is correct to condemn any facet of Manicheanism. However, not only is Manicheanism foreign to the teachings of all of Scripture, but the notion itself contradicts Scripture. Second, even if the Lordship of Christ and the example of the primitive church evinced in Scripture a "Christ against culture" pattern of discipleship, then such a pattern would be prescriptive for the modern church, not the other way around. Scripture stands in judgment of the modern church; the modern church does not stand in judgement of Scripture.

approach due to eschatology as Stott contends. Neither one of these approaches are adequate, much less congruent with Scripture's notion of the inauguration of the kingdom of God.

Also, some proponents of missional thinking have served as a corrective against apathetic abuses of some proponents of the traditional approach, where all that matters is the mandate of the Great Commission, where concerns for the physical well-being of the poor or victims of HIV are ignored. Missional thinking has served as an important corrective on this point. For the remainder of this chapter I will offer a very narrow and specific notion of missions: missions formed and informed by the inauguration and future consummation of the kingdom of God's new creation.

Missions is not holistic according to Stott, nor is missions missional according to Wright. If missions is broadly missional, then missions is nothing. Mission, namely the mission of the church, is narrow and specific, restricted to those actions and ministries taken on by the church to present, to witness, and to proclaim the gospel message of the kingdom of God's new creation to the unregenerate.

What Is Mission?

First, let us quickly define our terms. What is "mission(s)"?[70] The term itself is not a biblical word like "kingdom" or "Eschaton." However, as DeYoung and Gilbert note, "mission" is not precisely extrabiblical either because the Latin verb for "mission" is *mittere*, which corresponds to the Greek verb *apostellein*, which of course occurs in the New Testament 137 times, from which we get the noun "apostle": that is, one who is sent.[71] In our context, we are talking about the church being sent, the corporate body of Christ,

---

70. When I speak of missions, I'm speaking about the mission of the institutional church, which I will demonstrate to be narrow. However, there is a sense that missions is broad. This broad sense of missions is connected to the nature of individual Christian secular vocation(s). I prefer the term "missional" in regard to a Christian's vocation to glorify God by protologically transforming this world to reflect God's will as revealed in the Decalogue. Changing the world via Christian vocation is a blessed consequence of missions in the broad sense but it's not the mission of the church in the narrow sense. My project is not about Christian vocation and its broad missional approach to glorify God and change the culture for good. My project centers on the mission of the institutional church in making disciples (narrow approach) who will (as a consequence) then go out into the world as changed people to then change the culture based on their gifts and stations in life (broad, missional approach).

71. DeYoung and Gilbert, *What Is the Mission*, 17.

the visible, institutional church.⁷² Who is the one sending the church? Christ Jesus sends his church. As Bosch says, mission "... presupposes a sender, a person or persons sent by a sender, those who are sent, and an assignment."⁷³ The question we are addressing is: "what is Jesus sending His church to do, that it must or ought to do?"⁷⁴ And if the church does not fulfill her assignment, then it would be committing the sin of omission! This is where definition and precision matter. If definition and precision matter when defining the term "justification," then definition and precision matter when defining "mission." As Stephen Neill says, "If everything is mission then nothing is mission."⁷⁵

Great Commission Proof Texts

In contrast to what the church can do, what is the assignment that she is mandated to undertake? This takes us to the so-called Great Commission texts. The principal text we begin with is Matthew 28:16–20:

> Now the eleven disciples went to Galilee, to the mountain to which Jesus had directed them. And when they saw him they worshiped him, but some doubted. And Jesus came and said to them, "All authority in heaven and on earth has been given to me. Go therefore and make disciples of all nations, baptizing them in the name of the Father and of the Son and of the Holy Spirit, teaching them to observe all that I have commanded you. And behold, I am with you always, to the end of the age.

This famous Commission text begins with Jesus' directing his disciples to Galilee, that is, "to the mountain." Mountains are important places for the most important discourses given in the book of Matthew. Examples of this are from Sinai to the Sermon on the Mount in chapters 5–7, the Mount of Transfiguration in chapter 17, and the Olivet Discourse in chapter

---

72. A great discussion on the distinction between the church as organism and the church as institution is Kuyper, *Rooted and Grounded*.

73. Bosch, *Transforming Missions*, 1.

74. Stephen Neill makes allowance for a theology of ministry vis-à-vis a theology of missions, with the latter (as I will argue) defining mission as not everything the church can do. There is a broad scope of Christian activities that a church or Christian can do under the rubric of "ministry." However, in contrast to ministry, mission(s) is what the church ought to do. The church *can* do many things, but the church *must* do one thing. See Ferdinando, "Mission."

75. Quoted in DeYoung and Gilbert, *What Is the Mission*, 18.

Practical Implications

24—these are places of revelation.[76] Trent Rogers sees the "mountain of the Great Commission" against the backdrop of Second Temple Judaism's opposition vis-à-vis the authority of Christ. He says that "The mountain of the Great Commission serves as the culmination of the convergence of the Son of God and Moses themes throughout the Gospel in which Matthew argues that Jesus, the Son of God, is the only one to whom the community owes worship and obedience."[77] Rogers notes that in Second Temple Judaism, Moses was considered to have been not only a prophet and priest, but also a king; that is to say, Christ Jesus, who was considered by the Matthean community to be the greater king and lawgiver—that is, a greater king and lawgiver with greater authority and power—has the right to pass down to the New Testament church divine instruction as did Moses to his people. Rogers sees in the Great Commission the assertion of Christ's authority as the unique Son of God, drawing from Psalm 2.[78] Rogers says,

> . . . the Great Commission must be interpreted within the context of what Matthew is doing in the Gospel as a whole. As a continuation of the assertion of Jesus' preeminence in opposition to his opponents' assertion of Moses, Matthew subtly shows the Son's uniqueness by his claim. Jesus' claim of authority becomes clearer as an allusion to his Sonship drawing again on the Davidic king of Ps. 2. In both cases, God is the agent of δίδωμι and grants extensive authority to his Son, and the events of both scenes occur on a mountain.[79]

The allusion to Psalm 2 is significant. Earlier, during the baptism of Jesus at the Jordon River, Matthew (Roger contends) adopts ". . . Mark 1:11 which in turn draws from Ps. 2 and Isa. 42. Psalm 2 belongs to the category of coronation or enthronement psalms in which God enthrones his king on Mount Zion."[80]

The content of the Matthean Great Commission is generally understood to be constitutive of three parts: first, the proclamation of authority in verse 18b; second, the commission in versees 19–20a; third, the promise

---

76. For the significance of the mountain motif, see Donaldson, *Jesus on the Mountain*. Donaldson observes that the motif of the mountain is a primary theological setting for Jesus's ministry and teaching, serving to structure Matthew's narrative as it progresses.

77. Rogers, "Great Commission," 383.

78. Rogers, "Great Commission," 385; see also footnote 6.

79. Rogers, "Great Commission," 394–95.

80. Rogers, "Great Commission," 388.

Kingdom Theology

of abiding presence in verse 20b. Let's look at each in order. The first is the proclamation of authority in verse 18b. Donaldson says that there are striking verbal and conceptual similarities between Daniel and Matthew. Daniel 7:14 in the Septuagint reads, "And to him was given authority," and Matthew 28:18b—with the exception of the change in person in Matthew and the absence of πᾶσα in Daniel—reads, "All authority ... has been given to me."[81] In addition to that, both Daniel and Matthew also have "all the nations." There are conceptual similarities as well. The conceptual similarity of unlimited ἐξουσία in both Daniel and Matthew, and the explicit mention of gentiles subsumed under said sphere of authority, have led some scholars to the conclusion that Matthew 28:18–20 is an explicit fulfillment of Daniel 7:13f.[82] Donaldson sees it as possibly Matthew's "creative reinterpretation" of Daniel "... in order to present the post-resurrection commissioning as a proleptic *parousia*."[83] R. T. France points out that Jesus himself used the language of Daniel 7:13–14 to point to his own future sovereignty as God's vicegerent as the Son of Man. R. T. France says,

> Jesus himself, risen from the dead, is now revealed in all his glory as the vindicated and enthroned Son of Man, a status which he has hitherto spoken of only as a future expectation, but which has now become a reality.... [The] new international community will be his *ekklesia* (16:8) because it is he who now holds all authority in heaven and on earth (an authority greater than that which he was initially offered by Satan and refused, 4:8–10); [which is] the culmination of the theme of kingship.[84]

Jesus' universal authority is affirmed four times by the word "all" in verses 18–20, making a "final comprehensive declaration" by means of the Great Commission.[85]

In connection to Jesus' universal authority as God's vicegerent, the partial fulfillment of Matthew 28:18, as it echoes Daniel 7:14, indicates that

---

81. Donaldson, *Jesus on the Mountain*, 175.

82. See for example Ellis, *Matthew*, 23.

83. Donaldson, *Jesus on the Mountain*, 177. I would not call it a "creative reinterpretation," but an "authoritative interpretation." I take the middle ground between seeing Matt 28:18–20 as a complete, total fulfillment, on the one hand, and seeing it as a proleptic *parousia*, on the other hand. My reasoning is that because of Christ's inauguration of the kingdom, Matt 28:18–20 is a partial "already" fulfillment of Dan 7:13 and at the same time a "not yet" anticipation of the consummation of said kingdom.

84. France, *Gospel of Matthew*, 1108.

85. France, *Gospel of Matthew*, 1109.

Christ Jesus as the Son of Man ". . . is thus apparently linked with the vindication and enthronement of Jesus after the resurrection."[86] As France says, "It seems, then, that the sovereign authority envisioned in Daniel 7:13–14, first inaugurated when Jesus has risen from the dead, works itself out in successive phases throughout history until it finds its ultimate fulfillment in the last judgement."[87] Wilson sees in Jesus' "coming of the Son of Man" in Matthew 24, echoing Daniel 7:13–14, a Jesus ". . . bringing judgement on his contemporaries and their society" in AD 70 as being one phase in history, that is, an adumbration of the last judgment.[88] France says,

> It is this universal sovereignty that is the essential basis of the commission which is to follow in vv. 19–20, and thus of the continuing life of the disciple's community until the end of the age. . . . Here at the end of the gospel, then, we find the culmination of the theme of kingship which was introduced by the Davidic royal genealogy (1:1–17), developed in the magi's search for the "king of the Jews" and the political threat to Herod in chapter 2, adumbrated in the developing language of the Messiahship, and dramatically enacted in Jesus' royal ride into Jerusalem (21:1–11); since then Jesus' alleged claim to kingship has been a matter of accusation and mockery (27:11, 29, 37, 42), but now the true nature of that kingship is revealed. It stands far above political politics and extends far beyond the people of Israel. It is the universal kingship of the Son of Man which has emerged as a distinct feature of Matthew's presentation of Jesus: 13:41; 16:28; 19:28; 20:21; 25:31–34.[89]

France rhetorically asks, "Are we then to understand the 'coming of the Son of Man' [in Matt 28:18] as marking the end of a mission specifically to Israel, when universal kingship of the Son of Man is established after his resurrection and his church's mission is accordingly widened beyond the narrow bounds set in Matthew 10:5–6?"[90] The answer is yes! In short, based on both verbal and conceptual similarities, it is clear that the controlling factor in Matthew's echoing of Daniel in relation to the Great Commission in Jesus' proclamation of authority is the kingdom of God motif. The kingdom of God's inaugurated new creation is the controlling factor as it is

---

86. France, *Gospel of Matthew*, 397.
87. France, *Gospel of Matthew*, 397.
88. Wilson, *When Will These Things Happen?*, 61.
89. France, *Gospel of Matthew*, 1113.
90. France, *Gospel of Matthew*, 398.

Kingdom Theology

the source that forms and informs the Commission that Christ has given his church.

The second is the commission in verses 28:19–20a. The agents of the commission include disciples. In 24:30, Jesus envisions a future heavenly enthronement of the Son of Man, who will lead a mission to gather the elect from "the four winds, from one end of heaven to the other." The first part of Christ's vision has now been inaugurated in 28:18. The agents of the commission to gather God's elect are not only angels (the unseen realm, which is part of the divine strategy) but also the seen realm, that is, those who are already disciples of Jesus, which includes not only the original eleven disciples, but a larger number of committed disciples as their number increases. In short, the agents of the commission are under the jurisdiction of the kingdom of God and delimited by said jurisdiction by only disciples.

The scope of the commission is "all the nations." This phrase has occurred before in 24:9, 14; 25:32. France says that this "denote[s] the area of the disciples' future activity, the scope of the proclamation of the 'good news of the kingdom,' and the extent of the jurisdiction of the enthroned Son of Man."[91] Carson notes that the phrase "all the nations" is not excluding Israel, but simply going beyond Israel. Carson correctly hears an echo of the promise God gave to Abraham in Genesis 12:1–3, that all the nations will be blessed.[92] As James Boice, says, the scope of the commission ". . . refers, as I have just anticipated, to the universal authority of Jesus over all people and thus also to the worldwide character of Christianity."[93] In short, the scope of the commission is also under the jurisdiction of the kingdom of God.

The assignment of the commission is to "make disciples." The root of the main verb is μαθητεύω, which means to disciple or teach. This verb is in the imperative mood, that is, a command given by Christ as the newly inaugurated mediatorial king. This main verb is followed by two uncoordinated participles, namely "baptizing" and "teaching." These two participles spell out the means of making disciples: reaching and teaching. Reaching (evangelizing the unregenerate) and teaching the regenerate are the two means for making disciples.[94]

---

91. France, *Gospel of Matthew*, 1114.
92. Carson, "Matthew," 596.
93. Boice, *Gospel of Matthew*, 2:648.
94. France, *Gospel of Matthew*, 1115. France notes that the preceding third uncoordinated participle "going" is not a key element in the commission, that it's secondary to the

Practical Implications

The question regarding baptism that has to be asked is this: is the sacrament of baptism a graduation ceremony—a ceremony administered only after the catechumen has gone through sufficient instruction—or a rite of initiation? France affirms the latter:

> If the order of Matthew's participle is meant to be noticed, he is here presenting a different model whereby baptism is the point of enrollment into a process of learning which is never complete; the Christian community is a school of learners at various stages of development rather than dividing into the baptized (who have 'arrived') and those who are 'not yet ready.'[95]

Within the process of making disciples, baptism is an initiatory rite of those who have been reached and evangelized by the kingdom message of the gospel, a rite of passage from the kingdom of this age into the kingdom of God's inaugurated new creation.

Some have wondered if Jesus' instruction to baptize was the initial launch of Christian baptism, or if Christian baptism was in continuity with the Jesus movement, an adoption of John's practice of baptism for the expansion of missions to include the nations. This is open to debate.[96] However, it's clear that when it comes to the teaching role of making disciples, there is continuity between Jesus as teacher teaching his disciples and the disciples as teachers teaching their disciples. This is a decisive change marked by the death and resurrection of Christ Jesus. There is a close connection between Christ's authority and teaching. The disciples' duty to teach derives from the authority of Christ, the inaugurated mediatorial king, the authority to exercise the keys of the kingdom to not only baptize but to teach. As France says, "To be a disciple is to obey Jesus' teaching."[97]

What was the content of Jesus' teaching that was to be passed down by means of teaching the nations to obey or observe all that Jesus has commanded? In part, some of the content of Jesus' teaching is found in the Sermon on the Mount. John Nolland sees a connection between the call to repentance in light of the approaching kingdom in Matthew 4:17

---

both the main verb and the other two subordinate participles.

95. France, *Gospel of Matthew*, 1116. Also see Brow, *Go Make Disciples:*. Brow argues for a Matthean perspective of discipleship where baptism is an initiatory rite preceding instruction vis-à-vis graduation ceremony that precedes study.

96. France, *Gospel of Matthew*, 1116. France argues the latter is the most likely scenario, and I agree.

97. France, *Gospel of Matthew*, 1119.

and the teaching of the Sermon on the Mount. Nolland says, "The content of the coming address is appropriately identified as teaching rather than proclamation, but what Jesus is to say is to be thought of as grounded in his proclamation of the near approach of the kingdom of God and as clarifying what, for the disciple, lies beyond the repentance called for in 4:17."[98] Michael J. Wilkins says, concerning the Sermon on the Mount, that "He [that is, Matthew] has gathered together a collection of Jesus' messages[99] that enable the church for all ages to carry out a crucial component of Jesus' final commission: 'teaching them to obey everything I have commanded you' (28:20)."[100] Davies and Allison are correct when they note that,

> In [Matt] 5:1, the unspecified disciples, who must be a group larger than the four of 4:18–22, are—and this is the key point—contrasted with the crowd and so represent the church. The disciples, in other words, stand for the faithful; they are transparent symbols of believers. So the Sermon on the Mount is spoken directly to Matthew's Christian readers.[101]

However, to limit the content of teaching to particular teachings of Jesus—for example, the Sermon on the Mount or the Gospels—is to miss the larger point. Second Peter 3:3 explicitly teaches that the commandments of our Lord and Savior include all the teachings of the apostles, that it's through the apostles' teachings that Jesus commands his church. As Horton says,

> Being Christ's disciples means bringing people into the sphere of the church's ministry of preaching and sacrament. It involves being instructed not just in the basics of biblical teaching, but in everything Jesus commanded for our doctrine and life.[102]

In short, the specific mandate of the Great Commission depends on the gospel, the gospel as it's delivered through the means of grace; that is, Word, sacrament, and discipline. The good news is the means, and the assignment is the end; that is, proclaiming the message of the gospel of the inaugurated kingdom of new creation is for the purpose of making disciples. The

---

98. Nolland, *Gospel of Matthew*, 193.

99. With the exception of "gathering together a collection" instead of a sermon given by Jesus on a single occasion, I agree with the author.

100. Wilkins, "Original Meaning, Matthew," 190.

101. Davies and Allison, *Critical and Exegetical Commentary on Matthew*, 425.

102. Horton, *Gospel Commission*, 138.

proclamation of the gospel message of the kingdom of God's new creation to the nations is the process of making disciples. Missions is not being missional in the vein of Wright; and missions is not social action in the vein of Stott. Missions is, as Ferdinando contends, about making disciples, that is, reaching and teaching followers of Christ.[103] Missions is making disciples until the end of this age.

A second Great Commission text is Mark 13:10; 14:9: "And the gospel must first be proclaimed to all nations"; "And truly, I say to you, wherever the gospel is proclaimed in the whole world, what she has done will be told in memory of her."[104] Both of these texts predict that the gospel will and must be proclaimed throughout the world.

A third Great Commission text is Luke 24:44–49, which complements Matthew 28:16–20:

> Then he said to them, 'These are my words that I spoke to you while I was still with you, that everything written about me in the Law of Moses and the Prophets and the Psalms must be fulfilled.' Then he opened their minds to understand the Scriptures, and said to them, 'Thus it is written, that the Christ should suffer and on the third day rise from the dead, and that repentance for the forgiveness of sins should be proclaimed in his name to all nations, beginning from Jerusalem. You are witnesses of these things. And behold, I am sending the promise of my Father upon you. But stay in the city until you are clothed with power from on high.

As with Matthew, Luke grounds Jesus' command on divine authority. The difference is that unlike Matthew, who grounds the Great Commission mandate on the authority granted to Christ as the mediatorial king, Luke grounds said authority in Scripture. The disciples are to go forth because all authority has been given to Christ, and as a fulfillment of prophecy. The disciples' bearing witness in the power of the Holy Spirit is based on Christ's authority and Scripture. What is implied in Matthew 28:19 by "baptizing them" is made explicit in Luke 24:47: "repentance for the forgiveness of sins should be proclaimed in his name to all nations."

A fourth Great Commission text is Acts 1:8: "But you will receive power when the Holy Spirit has come upon you, and you will be my

---

103. Ferdinando, "Mission," 54.

104. Although Mark 16:15 is a post-resurrection Great Commission, it's not original to a Mark. However, it does represent a missionary impulse of the early church, which added it in the early second century. See DeYoung and Gilbert, *What Is the Mission*, 47.

witnesses in Jerusalem and in all Judea and Samaria, and to the end of the earth." Like Matthew, Acts emphasizes the nations, that is, "Samaria and the ends of the earth," while not excluding Jerusalem and Judea. Like Luke, the major theme of Spirit-empowered witness is central in Acts. As DeYoung and Gilbert note, preaching and teaching and the importance of the Word in the power of the Spirit are the means within the entire book of Acts of carrying out the Great Commission given in Acts 1:8.[105]

A fifth Great Commission text is John 20:21: "Jesus said to them again, 'Peace be with you. As the Father has sent me, even so I am sending you.'" Three theological points are highlighted here.[106] First, Jesus gives his disciples peace. Peace is not society renewal, but reconciliation and fellowship with God. For example, in John 14:26–27 peace is the assurance that the Holy Spirit will always be with his disciples. In John 16:33, such peace is found exclusively in Christ. In short, the peace Jesus bestows is the peace that comes from the forgiveness of sins and the reconciliation of sinful man with a holy God. Second, Jesus' mission is prior to our mission; Jesus is sent first, then he sends us! There is continuity and discontinuity between Jesus' being sent and our being sent by Jesus. Jesus' mission is foundational to our mission. There is an analogy of functionality. In short, the mission of Jesus is carried on by his followers. Third, Jesus' mission is a model for our mission. As DeYoung and Gilbert contend, "Our role is to bear witness to what Christ has already done . . . [as] his representatives offering life in his name, proclaiming his gospel, imploring others to be reconciled to God."[107]

Conclusion

In light of these Great Commission texts, there is room for diversity: Matthew's accent is on making disciples. Both Luke and Acts emphasize being witnesses. John highlights the analogy between Christ being sent first, then Christ sending us. However, these texts are in harmony. Though there are Great Commission texts, there is but one Great Commission.[108] What constitutes the Great Commission? First, the Great Commission is a mandate

---

105. DeYoung and Gilbert, *What Is the Mission*, 49.

106. DeYoung and Gilbert, *What Is the Mission*, 49. Much of what I will share is from pages 52–58.

107. DeYoung and Gilbert, *What Is the Mission*, 57.

108 DeYoung and Gilbert, *What Is the Mission*, 57. My constitutive summary is from page 59.

given to Christ's first disciples, and then passed down to all followers of Christ to the end of this age. Second, the mandate consists of proclaiming and preaching the gospel message of the inaugurated, new-creational kingdom of God (evangelism) and teaching this kingdom message to the disciples so they may obey the commandments of the king (that is, making disciples), and to testify and bear witness to this present kingdom. Third, this proclamation and teaching and testifying and bearing witness to the kingdom of God are rooted in the authority of the Old Testament, in the authority of God the Father sending forth his Son, and under the authority of Christ's mediatorial kingship, mediatorial in the sense of Christ being God's vicegerent! Fourth, the scope of this mandate is to all the nations, all the people groups irrespective of race or ethnicity, that is, an ethnic universalism. Fifth, the power that enables us to go out is the power of the Holy Spirit, in submission to the Son and the Father. Sixth, the Great Commission was inaugurated at Pentecost when the Holy Spirit baptized the disciples with power on high with spiritual gifts! In short, contrary to both Stott and Wright, the mandate of the Great Commission is narrow and very specific, narrowly defined and limited and circumscribed to what must be done! This mandate is restricted to those actions and ministries taken on by the church to present, to witness, and to proclaim the gospel message of the kingdom of God's new creation by harvesting, gathering, and perfecting the elect. As DeYoung and Gilbert also conclude, "The mission of the church is to go into the world and make disciples by declaring the gospel of Jesus Christ in the power of the Spirit and gathering these disciples into churches, that they might worship the Lord and obey his commands now and in eternity to the glory of God the Father."[109]

THE INAUGURATED KINGDOM AND ITS IMPLICATION FOR THE CHURCH

So far, it has been demonstrated that the mandate of the Great Commission is the essential mission of the church, and that mission is very specific and narrowly defined, limited and circumscribed. Scripture clearly describes that it is narrow. But the question is: why? Why is the mandate of the Great Commission narrowly defined and circumscribed? This is where the notion of the kingdom of God comes in play. It's the inauguration of the new-creational kingdom that circumscribes missions. The implication of

109. DeYoung and Gilbert, *What Is the Mission*, 62.

Kingdom Theology

the inaugurated new-creational kingdom is that the mission of the church is narrow and very specific to said lineaments. This is the essence of the doctrine of the spirituality of the church.

The First Adamic State of the Cultural Mandate

But the question is: how does this work? How does the inaugurated new-creational kingdom narrow the mission of the church, a narrowing that is clearly demonstrated in the Great Commission texts? Another way to pose the question is to ask: why is the Great Commission of the church narrowly focused? What is it about the inaugurated new-creational kingdom that causes the repercussion or implication of the mandate of the Great Commission to be so narrowly focused? In order to connect the dots, let's begin with the two great federal heads of humanity and human history: the first Adam and the last Adam. Romans 5 and 1 Corinthians 15 both teach that humanity's fate depends on both the first and last Adam. VanDrunen observes that the doctrine of the two Adams is the "hinge upon which all history turns."[110] As I shared earlier, the purpose of history is about the sovereign plan of God to unite all things again under one domain, one kingdom—namely, to unite all things in Christ and to put all things under his feet (Eph 1:22). The meta-purpose is to reinstate and reestablish the eschatological kingdom of God in Christ, a kingdom that Adam abdicated. I also noted earlier that Jesus' inauguration of the kingdom in the Gospels, and throughout the New Testament, is to be understood as "the reinstatement of the originally intended divine order for earth, with man properly situated as God's vicegerent."[111] McCartney points out that in the original kingship, Adam "spoiled his vicegerency." This "reinstatement of the original prelapsarian order" goes beyond the original order or original kingdom; "it's an advancement over the Adamic state."[112]

How is Christ's reinstatement of the original vicegerency an advancement over the Adamic state? This comes down to understanding the nature of the original cultural mandate. VanDrunen is most insightful on this point.[113] Earlier, in my second chapter, I noted that the kingdom of God

---

110. VanDrunen, *Living in God's Two Kingdoms*, 50.

111. McCartney, "Ecce Homo," 2.

112. McCartney, "Ecce Homo," 2.

113. Much of what I will share concerning Christ fulfilling the cultural mandate originally given to Adam is informed by VanDrunen's *Living in God's Two Kingdoms*, 35–71.

Practical Implications

has a spatial component to it: that is, it originally was the garden-temple of Eden. The garden-temple was the spatial location of the kingdom of God, where both cult and culture were integrated.[114] Also, earlier I noted that God created man in his image; in Genesis 5:3 "image" means man as son, and son means king, making man as image of God also mean son of God as king. In the original creation, God ruled the earth by way of the kingship of man's vicegerency. The image of God is moral and rational; that is, the *imago Dei* has both an ontological and functional dimension to it. Adam was created in the image of God in order to function as king. It seems logical to say the functional (God's vicegerent) presupposes the ontological. Adam was a volitional, rational, moral agent/creature who reflected God's volitional, rational, moral agency as Creator.

VanDrunen says that the New Testament gives us some clues on how to authoritatively interpret Genesis 1:26–27. Ephesians 4:24 and Colossians 3:10 teach that by faith in Christ Christians are being renewed in the image of God. This means that the image that Christ is renewing is by definition not new; it was the original constitution of man. Man was originally constituted in terms of "knowledge" (Col 3:10) and "righteousness" and "holiness" (Eph 4:24). As VanDrunen says, these are "moral and rational capabilities put to good use. Thus Paul indicates that bearing God's image is about *who we are* and especially *what we do*."[115] The ontological made it possible for Adam to function as the divine vicegerent. As God's vicegerent, Adam was to exercise dominion; this exercise of dominion was a function of being in the image and likeness of God.

Adam was given both the office of king and a commission. Unlike the rest of creation, Adam, as a rational creature in the likeness and image of God, was obligated and accountable to God. That accountability was instantiated in Genesis 1:26: "Then God said, 'Let us make man in our image, after our likeness. And let them have dominion over the fish of the sea and over the birds of the heavens and over the livestock and over all the earth and over every creeping thing that creeps on the earth.'" The exercise or function of dominion is at the heart and the very nature of being made in the image of God; Adam was created in the image of God in order to have

---

114. Irons, "Meredith Kline's View," 6. Irons notes that the nature of Kline's integration is based on the prelapsarian "theocratic principle" where culture is subordinate to the cult. By "culture" Kline means the act of worship, with special focus on priestly work of offering tribute to God in the temple.

115. VanDrunen, *Living in God's Two Kingdoms*, 38.

Kingdom Theology

dominion.[116] Adam's dominion, under the dominion of God, is more like God than other works of other creatures. As VanDrunen says, "God made Adam to be a wise, holy, and righteous king. He was to pick up where God left off."[117] Just as God names many of the creatures (for example, Gen 1:5, 8, 10), likewise Adam was to name those that had not been named by God (for example, 2:19–20). Also, just as God created the first human being by means of supernatural generation, likewise Adam and Eve's commission was to procreate by means of natural generation, and populate the world with a multitude of image-bearing descendants (1:28). VanDrunen sums it up nicely by saying, "The first Adam was made in the divine image as the royal son of God, commissioned to exercise wise, righteous, and holy dominion over the world."[118] Middleton says,

> The description of ancient Near Eastern kings as the image of god, when understood as an integral component of Egyptian and/or Mesopotamian royal ideology, provides the most plausible set of parallels for the interpreting the *imago Dei* in Genesis 1. If such texts . . . influence the biblical *imago Dei*, this suggests that humanity is dignified with a status and role vis-à-vis the nonhuman creation that is analogous to the status and role of kings in the ancient Near East royal ideologies. As *imago Dei*, then, humanity in Genesis 1 is called to be the representative and intermediary of God's power and blessing on earth.[119]

But there is a third imitation of dominion: Adam was not only to image God's likeness by exercising dominion by means of naming the many creatures and procreation, but also to imitate God's pattern of work and rest. Just as God worked for six days and after accomplishing his work rested from creating, likewise Adam's mandate of the original commission was to work and rest as God, that is, to consummate his work and rest from all his labor. As VanDrunen says, "The first Adam did not bear God's image in order to work aimlessly in the original creation and to sit down enthroned in a royal-rest."[120]

---

116. VanDrunen, *Living in God's Two Kingdoms*, 39. VanDrunen notes that the grammar of the original Hebrew text likely indicates a purpose clause. See his footnote 2.

117. VanDrunen, *Living in God's Two Kingdoms*, 39.

118. VanDrunen, *Living in God's Two Kingdoms*, 40.

119. Middleton, *Liberating Image*, 121.

120. VanDrunen, *Living in God's Two Kingdoms*, 40.

Practical Implications

What confirmation do we have that Adam's original cultural/dominion mandate of Genesis 1:26–28 was a task of definite duration, working toward a final end or purpose? Hebrews 2:5–8 is clear that Adam was to complete his task in this world and to enter victoriously in the world to come. Hebrews 2:5 says, "For it was not to angels that God subjected the world to come, of which we are speaking." Guthrie notes that the negative statement by the author of Hebrews (that is, "not to angels that God subjected the world to come") "is vital to our understanding of how he uses this passage from the OT."[121] The author of Hebrews quotes Psalm 8[122] to prove that God's original mandate for Adam was for man to be ruler over all things, leading up to and culminating with the "world to come." Man's original destiny, prior to the fall, was to rule in the age to come "as a participation in God's seventh-day rest of Genesis 2:1–3," a destiny accomplished only by Christ in Hebrews 4:1–10.[123] The original context for Psalms 8 is the stewardship given to man, that is, man's dominion over creation; this dominion was not just man in general, but Adam in particular with the motif of "Adamic kingship being squarely in focus . . . [communicating] a divine, ongoing commission . . . [of] repeated failure to fulfill that commission by Adam, Noah, Israel . . ."[124] As Irons says,

> Man's weekly Sabbath cycle was not to be indefinite or never ending. Rather, it was part of the covenant of works, and therefore the weekly Sabbath contained an eschatological promise. The weekly sign of the Sabbath was a token to Adam that his cultural activity of procreating, filling the earth and subduing it would, or (more accurately) could, come to a consummation, the consummation of entering God's Sabbath rest. Man had the hope that, just as God's creation activity came to a conclusion and God rested on the seventh day, so man's cultural activity could one day be completed and he, together with all his progeny, and all of creation itself, would be ushered into the eschatological Sabbath rest of God himself.[125]

VanDrunen nicely summarizes the teaching of Hebrews 2:5–8 regarding the world to come as new creation:

---

121. Guthrie, "Hebrews," 944.

122. Guthrie, "Hebrews," 945. Guthrie says, "In [Psalm] 8:5–8 we find a reflection on Genesis 1:26–28, where God commissions human beings, created in the image of God, to rule . . ."

123. VanDrunen, *Living in God's Two Kingdoms*, 45.

124. Guthrie, "Hebrews," 945.

125. Irons, "Meredith Kline's View," 5.

> [Adam] was not only to be like God in exercising royal dominion in the original creation, but was to enter royal rest as ruler of the new creation. He was to follow the pattern of his God, who did magnificent work in this world for six days and then sat down enthroned on the seventh day. He could look forward to partaking of the tree of life (Genesis 2:9), which was not the symbol of life upon earth, but life in the new heavens and new earth (Revelation 22:2).[126]

And since Adam is humanity's federal head according to Romans 5:12–19, then we can logically deduce that Adam's posterity would have shared in the original cultural/dominion mandate to rule over the world to come as well.

However, the question must be asked: what criteria would have Adam met to demonstrate that he had finished his task? What were the conditions? VanDrunen says that Genesis 2 provides the answer. In Genesis 1:26–28, God gave Adam broad, general commands with regard to the world; in contrast, in 2:15–17 God gives Adam very narrow, precise commands regarding a very specific part of the world, that is, the garden of Eden. God commands Adam "to work and keep it." Also, God gives Adam a specific negative command. God commands Adam not to eat from the tree of death, that is, the knowledge of good and evil. The garden of Eden, in contrast to the rest of the world, was the holy dwelling place of God, that is, the temple of God.[127] It's in the garden of Eden that God puts Adam to the test to see whether he will be a vicegerent who will reign faithfully in this world and the world to come, or unfaithfully. Adam's general obligation in Genesis 1 is tested in Genesis 2. As VanDrunen says, "While Genesis 1:26–28 requires Adam to serve as a king, Genesis 2:15 requires Adam to serve both as king and as a priest."[128] In Genesis 2:15, God mandates that Adam is to "work" and "keep" the garden. Many contemporary writers contextualize "work" to refer to the building of human civilization, and "keep" to refer to ecological stewardship. Case in point is Pearcey when she says,

> The first phrase, "be fruitful and multiply," means to develop the social world: build families, churches, schools, cities, governments, laws. The second phrase, "subdue the earth," means to harness the

126. VanDrunen, *Living in God's Two Kingdoms*, 41. Also see Guthrie, "Hebrews," 956–60.

127. See Beale, *Temple and the Church's Mission*, 70–76. Beale gives biblical evidence that many of the features of the biblical text indicate that the garden was a temple.

128. VanDrunen, *Living in God's Two Kingdoms*, 42.

Practical Implications

natural world: plant crops, build bridges, design computers, and compose music. This passage is sometimes called the Cultural Mandate because this passage tells us that our original purpose was to create cultures, build civilizations—nothing less.[129]

But is this the main point, or the point at all? Is the main point about building human civilization and ecological stewardship? By overcontextualizing based upon a categorical misapplication,[130] one can come to such an anachronistic conclusion, making it not the main point nor the point at all. The main point is that Adam was to exercise not only royal dominion, but also exercise sacerdotal service. The garden of Eden was a temple where Adam as priest did his sacerdotal labor of working and keeping in the context of eschatological dominion and transformation. As Beale says, "Adam was to be like Israel's later priest, who both physically protected the temple and spiritually were to be experts in the recollection, interpretation, and application of God's word in the Torah."[131] Adam's commission to work and keep the garden was a priestly function as well as kingly.[132] In fact, the Hebrew words for "work" and "keep" are used in the Old Testament to refer to priestly labor. To "keep" is to guard the holy tabernacle. To guard the garden is a priestly act of guarding the garden against defilement.[133]

In short, Adam's royal task in Genesis 1 and Adam's royal priestly task in Genesis 2 are inseparable; that is, Adam's mandate to guard the garden in Genesis 2 was Adam's first step in realizing his mandate of worldwide dominion and transformation over all of creation in Genesis 1. As VanDrunen summarizes,

> He would have to assert his authority over this creature and protect the garden purity. This God was going to bring Adam's obligation into focus to test his obedience. Would he obey God? Would he be a faithful king under God's authority? Would he protect the purity of God's holy presence from anything that might defile it? Adam's probation in Eden would determine the answers.[134]

---

129. Pearcey, *Total Truth*, 50.

130. What I mean by "categorical misapplication" is that the original cultural mandate is under the eschatological category of redemption and transformation, not a protological category of preservation.

131. Beale, *New Testament Biblical Theology*, 33.

132. Beale, *New Testament Biblical Theology*, 32.

133. See Beale, *Temple and the Church's Mission*, 66–69, 84–85, 87.

134. VanDrunen, *Living in God's Two Kingdoms*, 43.

God makes a covenant with Adam, a covenant of works.[135] This covenant of works was a conditional promise. The promise was the reception of an eschatological reward of eternal life and transformative new creation, that is, dominion in the world to come. This promise was suspended on the condition of perfect and personal obedience. If Adam was disobedient, he would merit death and lose his reward. Adam, as both king and priest, was to assert his authority over Satan, and protect the garden's purity over and against Satan's usurpation of authority and threat of defiling the holiness of the garden.

God destined Adam (along with his posterity) to rule over not only this world, but the world to come. How are we doing? In Hebrews 2:8, the author bemoans the fact that not only has man not fulfilled his destiny to rule the world to come, but "at present we do not yet see everything in subjection to him," that is, Adam and his posterity. Hebrews 2:8 is in respect to what the author just said prior in 2:5, that is, the world to come. In other words, at present, in this age, man is inept and maladroit when it comes to the natural and social forces of this world. Far from man transforming the world, the world is conforming man; and far from man dominating the world, man is dominated, not capable of dominating this world, much less the world to come.

How can this be? Genesis 3 describes the etiology of the present failure of man. In Genesis 3 a new character is introduced: the serpent. Revelation 12:9 identifies the serpent as the devil. The serpent deceives Eve (according to 1 Tim 2:14) and persuades her to eat from the tree of death, that is, the tree of the knowledge of good and evil. He deceives and persuades her first by rebelling against the trustworthiness of God's Word. Satan declares, "You shall not surely die." Satan downplays the gravity of relinquishing or abdicating man's vicegerency. Why did man so easily abdicate his vicegerency, his God-given and endowed right to exercise dominion? The reason is Satan promised man something better than mere vicegerency. The offer was that by rebelling against God's command, man could be autonomous as God; that is, "You will be like God" (Gen 3:5). Why be penultimate if you could be ultimate! Why be a steward when you could be lord and master? Within five short tragic verses Satan deceives and persuades the woman, and in turn Eve tempts Adam to eat from the tree of autonomy, that is,

---

135. This insight into the covenant of work is in agreement with the Westminster Confession of Faith 7.2. Also see a contemporary defense in Fesko, *Justification*, 108–22.

the tree of death (Gen 3:6). What do these five short verses demonstrate? VanDrunen says,

> Genesis 3 confirms that Adam's general commission to exercise royal dominion was to focus specifically on the garden and would be tested through the tree of the knowledge of good and evil. It clarifies that the command about the tree (2:16–17) was not simply to an arbitrary requirement unrelated to Adam's general obligation to exercise dominion (1:26, 28). The tree of the knowledge of good and evil did not test Adam's willingness to obey an arbitrary divine command, but tested how faithfully he would exercise dominion by guarding the purity of the holy garden.[136]

Satan came in not only as a deceiver to tempt Adam to abdicate the throne by offering him something more than stewardship, but Satan was also an intruder who defiled the garden-temple. Instead of fulfilling his task as both king and priest—that is, to rule over the serpent by expelling him from the garden—Adam relinquished his dominion, and he let the serpent have dominion over him and defile the garden! In short, Adam did more than just simply disobey God's positive law of not eating of the tree of good and evil in Genesis 2, but he disobeyed the dominion/cultural mandate of Genesis 1, allowing the serpent to be king of God's creation (see Matt 4:8–9). And not only did Adam abdicate his kingship/kingdom, he also shunned his priesthood by allowing the serpent to defile the holy garden-temple.

What evidence do we have to demonstrate this particular reading of these five short verses depicting the fall? The answer is that the common curse in Genesis 3 strikes at the points where obedience was demanded.[137] First, regarding dominion, God commanded in Genesis 1 that man was to having dominion instantiated by being "fruitful and multiplying." What is the relationship between the dominion mandate, in Genesis 1, and the mandate to be fruitful and multiply in Genesis 2? Adam was to be fruitful and multiply not merely for the penultimate reason to fill the earth with his progeny—which is an aspect formally reinstated in the Noahic covenant in Genesis 8:20—9:17, where God pledges to preserve the stability of nature, a stability that will allow his people to flourish and that will provide an arena for the Christ to enter history and bring the salvation promised in Genesis 3:15—but Adam was to be fruitful and multiply for a higher, ultimate reason; the reason was to fill the earth with glory-image-bearing

---

136. VanDrunen, *Living in God's Two Kingdoms*, 44.
137. VanDrunen, *Living in God's Two Kingdoms*, 45–46.

Kingdom Theology

progeny, progeny who will glorify God to the fullest by their image-bearing presence. As Beale says,

> Ancient Near Eastern kings were considered to be "sons" of their god and to represent the image of their god in their rule, especially reflecting the god's glory and, accordingly, the manifestation of its presence. In fact, the images of gods in Mesopotamia and Egypt were intended to represent the god and manifest its presence.[138]

It was at this point that the curse of Genesis 3 strikes. God says in 3:16, "I will surely multiply your pain in childbearing; in pain you shall bring forth children." As VanDrunen says, "This curse falls on the primary activities—being fruitful and multiplying—that was to characterized human dominion over this world."[139] Second, God cursed the man again at the point of dominion. In 2:15, Adam was commanded to "work and keep" the garden. As "Lord of the land and the guardian of purity," Adam was mandated to work and keep it.[140] However, God curses the land: "cursed is the ground because of you; in pain you shall eat of it all the days of your life; thorns and thistles it shall bring forth for you; and you shall eat of the plant of the field. By the sweat of your face you shall eat bread . . ." (3:17–19). Third, God cursed man with death. God says, "till you return to the ground, for out of it you were taken; for you are dust, and to dust you shall return" (3:19). Death will frustrate Adam's original destiny of dominion in the world to come. Adam will return to the dust of this age without consummation in the age to come. In short, the curse makes it impossible for man to glorify God as an image-bearer by means of dominion over this world and the world to come. The ontological image of God is not annihilated. What is annihilated is man's glory-image-bearing ability to glorify God in his capacity to achieve dominion in this world and the world to come. Whatever image-bearing ability man still possesses in his cultural activities and pursuits after the fall, that ability is no longer a glory-image-bearing ability; it no longer brings glory to God. It is now a bare image-bearing ability that no longer brings God glory. Man has tragically lost his divine glory!

What New Testament teaching justifies this tragic reading? Romans 3:23 is a case in point. When Paul says in Romans 3:23 that "all have sinned and fallen short of the glory of God," Paul means to say is that man lacks (and will always fall short or lack) in his capacity to glorify God by means

---

138. VanDrunen, *Living in God's Two Kingdoms*, 36–37.
139. VanDrunen, *Living in God's Two Kingdoms*, 45.
140. VanDrunen, *Living in God's Two Kingdoms*, 45.

Practical Implications

of fulfilling his divine commission of dominion. Simply, man has sinned and lacks the glory of God. The Greek ὑστερέω, meaning "to fall short" (and interpreted in most translation as "fallen short"), can also be translated as "are lacking" or "are missing."[141] That is to say, instead of man falling short of God's objective standard, that is, inherent glory as a righteous standard, man is subjectively lacking or missing within himself the glory that God has stamped within man at creation. Just as the moon reflects the resplendent glory (light) of the sun, likewise man was created to reflect the resplendent glory of God. The former is a derivative of the latter, which is inherent.

What is the particular glory that man is lacking or missing that God originally vested in man, that is, man made in his image? For Paul, the glory of God is also instantiated in the *imago Dei*, making both glory and image synonymous terms. Prelapsarian man was full of the glory of God as man imitated and imaged God.[142] As Ortlund says,

> Generally speaking in Paul, the glory of God refers to God's own resplendence, magnificence, weightiness, honor. What we must bear in mind here is that Paul often speaks of δόξα not simply as God's own glory but as God's glory implanted upon humans—in essence, that is, the image of God. Where in the cosmos is God's glory actually, tangibly, seen and felt? In the created order, to be sure (Ps 19:1), but more particularly in humans, the rulers of the created order.[143]

What is that divine commission given to glorify God that man falls short in? It's his falling short as an image-bearer in having dominion over this world and the world to come. It's impossible for man to fulfill his destiny. When Adam relinquished his kingdom, he thwarted his destiny of new creation; that is, he relinquished and thwarted the kingdom of God's new creation! Dane Ortlund is correct when he sees in Romans 3:23 more than a mere affirmation of the universality of sin. Romans 3:23 is saying something much more profound than man not living up to the standard of God's glory, that is, God's own inherent perfect resplendence. Paul means more. Paul means, "that all of humanity sinned in Adam's sin, and as a result we are lacking the

---

141. Danker et al., *Greek-English Lexicon* (BDAG), 1044. BDAG endorses lacking, wanting, deficient, or missing vis-à-vis falling short. An example of this is from Mark 10:21, where the young ruler "lacked" the merit to earn salvation, i.e., living up to the righteous, moral demands of the law to earn or merit eternal life.

142. Beale, *New Testament Biblical Theology*, 456.

143. Ortlund, "What Does It Mean," 129.

fullness of the image of God with which we were originally vested in Eden. The meaning of the text could be rendered: 'All sinned [in Adam], and are thus lacking the glory-image of God.'"[144] Ortlund understands Romans 3:23 within the larger historical-redemptive framework of inaugurated eschatology under the two representative heads of humanity: the first and second Adam. He says,

> Paul has in mind God's glory as vested upon humans made in his image. When Paul says "all sinned" (an aorist and not, as many translations may lead one to think, a perfect) he means exactly what he will unpack two chapters later—in Adam, "all sinned" (5:12). I further suggest that the meaning of the rest of the verse is that sin has caused us to lack in some degree the glory of God— that is, the divine glory with which humanity was stamped in Eden, the imago dei, was defaced, disfigured, deformed.[145]

In short, not only is the ontological/essential nature that constitutes the glory-image of God in man corrupted—that is, defaced, disfigured, and deformed—lacking in some degree the glory of God, but what's also lacking is man's capacity for achieving dominion (the functional capacity of the image of God); that is lost. The essential/substantive nature of the *imago Dei* is not totally gone; it's disfigured. What is totally lost, gone, or annihilated is man's capacity for achieving dominion, a dominion that glorifies God.[146] As Beale says, "Adam . . . ceased to reflect God's glory after sin . . . he did not lose the divine image altogether, but it did become distorted losing the

---

144. Ortlund, "What Does It Mean," 121.

145. Ortlund, "What Does It Mean," 124.

146. Ortlund, "What Does It Mean," 130. Ortlund says, "Reading υστεροῦνται as 'are lacking' and 'the glory of God' as God's vested glory-image is not to suggest that the image is entirely gone, but rather that it is critically disfigured. In Gen 9, after the fall into sin, murder is prohibited on the grounds that mankind is God's image (Gen 9:6). Therefore the image cannot have been entirely lost in Adam's sin." I concur that the image is present, just not the glory-image. Scripture is clear that sinful, postlapsarian man lost the capacity to glorify God. If man has lost the capacity to glorify God (which is the standard of true charity toward God and man) that means the glory-image vested in man is entirely gone. This doesn't mean the essential/substantive element of the *imago Dei* is gone. Fallen man is in the substantive image of God. But because the substantive element is corrupted and disfigured, this in turn annihilates the functional element of the image, the glory-image. The glory-image is mutated into a bare image. Man can no longer function in his capacity to glorify via dominion. Just as the New Moon no longer reflects the glory of the Son, likewise the image of God in man no longer reflects the glory of God."

glorious aspect of that image."[147] The defacing and disfiguring and deforming of the substantial nature of the *imago Dei* abrogates the functional aspect of the *imago Dei*, which is the capacity for achieving dominion, a dominion that is God's glory implanted in man. As Ortlund says,

> Generally speaking in Paul, the glory of God refers to God's own resplendence, magnificence, weightiness, honor. What we must bear in mind here is that Paul often speaks of δόξα not simply as God's own glory but as God's glory implanted upon humans—in essence, that is, the image of God. Where in the cosmos is God's glory actually, tangibly, seen and felt? In the created order, to be sure (Ps 19:1), but more particularly in humans, the rulers of the created order.[148]

Humanity is how God makes his glory visible. In Adam we are sinners who continue to lack in making God's glory visible by having lost the capacity for achieving dominion, a dominion that reveals God's glory! In short, Romans 3:23 is teaching that, at present, man lacks within himself the glory of God (that is, man's loss of divine glory), because man lacks the capacity to achieve dominion in this world and the world to come!

The Second Adamic State of the Cultural Mandate

This doesn't mean that the cultural activity of man came to an end after the fall. In part, the creation/cultural mandate to be fruitful and multiply, as noted, has a bare, penultimate purpose as is true for all of man's cultural pursuits. Adam was to be fruitful and multiply so as to fill the earth with his progeny—which is an aspect formally reinstated in the Noahic covenant in Genesis 8:20—9:17, where God pledges to preserve (not transform and redeem) the stability of nature by means of common grace (not special grace), a stability that will allow God's people to flourish and that will provide an arena for the Christ to enter history and bring the salvation promised in Genesis 3:15. The fact is that after the fall all the cultural activities of fallen, unregenerate men are plagued with sin and failure. In this fallen state, man's cultural activities do not bring glory to God, but glory to man. Case in point is the Tower of Babel in Genesis 11:3–4:

---

147. Beale, *New Testament Biblical Theology*, 456.
148. Ortlund, "What Does It Mean," 124.

> "Come, let us make bricks, and burn them thoroughly." And they had brick for stone, and bitumen for mortar. Then they said, "Come, let us build ourselves a city and a tower with its top in the heavens, and let us make a name for ourselves, lest we be dispersed over the face of the whole earth."

Nimrod builds the first great civilization, the ancient city of Babylon. What was the purpose of this first great postdiluvian cultural activity? The purpose was to "make a name for ourselves," that is, for the glory of man, a glory doomed to destruction in this age (see Rev 18), never able to attain the new creation in the world to come. In short, no matter how "much fallen human beings may strive to pick up the baton from Adam and pursue the tasks of culture with an eye to an eternal prize, the quest is futile. They will end up not enthroned with God in glory, but condemned with the serpent in the lake of fire (Revelation 20:10, 14–15)."[149]

However, in Genesis 3:15, God promises a redeemer, the second Adam, to bring to completion what the first Adam failed to do. What Adam failed to do—that is, to perfectly obey the cultural mandate to glorify God in his capacity to achieve dominion in this world and the world to come—the second and last Adam has accomplished. Christ has attained man's original destiny on behalf of those whom are in Christ.

How exactly did Christ perfectly accomplish Adam's original task? Just as Adam's general mandate in Genesis 1 was tested in Genesis 2—that is, it's in the garden of Eden, where God puts Adam to the test to see whether he will be a faithful vicegerent who will reign faithfully in this world and the world to come, or unfaithfully—likewise it was for Christ. Adam's general obligation in Genesis 1 is tested in Genesis 2. Just as it was with Adam's mandate to guard the garden in Genesis 2, which was Adam's first step in realizing his mandate of worldwide dominion over all of creation in Genesis 1, so it was with Christ Jesus. During Jesus' earthly ministry, Jesus did not fill the earth with his progeny or exercise dominion over all creatures. VanDrunen says it this way:

> But as considered . . . Adam was to have his entire obedience in the entire world determined through a particular location. So it was for the last Adam. Like the first Adam, the Lord Jesus was confronted by the devil who tried to entice him (Matthew 4:1–11; Colossians 2:15; Hebrews 2:14). Like the first Adam, the Lord Jesus was called to priestly service, and Christ the Great High Priest

---

149. VanDrunen, *Living in God's Two Kingdoms*, 46–47.

Practical Implications

purified God's holy dwelling and opened the way for human beings back in presence (Hebrews 9:11–28; 10:19–22). Like the first Adam, the Lord Jesus was to enter God's royal rest in the world-to-come upon finishing his work perfectly, and this is precisely what Christ did, entering into heaven itself, taking his seat at God's right hand, ministering in the heavenly tabernacle, and securing our place in the world-to-come (Hebrews 1:3; 4:14–16; 7:23–28).[150]

The last Adam perfectly accomplished the task originally given to the first Adam. In Jesus' life, death, resurrection, and ascension he crushed the head of Satan as the righteous priest and king in this world, attaining the destiny—that is, entering into glory in the world to come—that Adam failed to do. In light of this second Adamic state accomplished by Christ Jesus, this Adamic state is imputed to believers. Believers, who are united with Christ, claim the victory of Christ as their own and are "already" citizens of the world to come, though "not yet" residents until Christ comes to consummate his kingdom.

Mission Accomplished

Some questions must be posed. First, how did Christ accomplish all of this? Second, how do believers share in the glory of the world to come? Regarding the former, Romans 5, 1 Corinthians 15, and Hebrews 2 address this. Romans 5:12–19 emphasizes that Christ obeyed God with perfect righteousness. Paul is explicit when he identifies the first Adam as the source of damnation, death, and sin that threw this age into chaos. In Romans 5:15, Paul speaks of "one man's trespasses." In 5:16, it's "one man's sin." In 5:19, it's "one man's disobedience." Paul's point is clear: one man in light of one act at one particular time in history plunged this world, this age into moral, natural, spiritual chaos and destruction. In contradistinction, Christ, who is the second Adam, the second federal head, was obedient, obeying God the Father in this age during his entire life, culminating in his crucifixion! The point is simple: where Adam failed, Christ accomplished. Adam was supposed to obey, displaying the glory of God by having dominion in this world and attaining eternal life. Jesus did obey; Jesus did display the glory of God by having dominion over sin and attaining eternal life!

In 1 Corinthians 15, Christ is the last Adam. The accent in 1 Corinthian 15 is on how Christ, as the last Adam, attained the destiny held out

---

150. VanDrunen, *Living in God's Two Kingdoms*, 50.

Kingdom Theology

to the first Adam under the covenant of works. In chapter 15 Paul explains at length the importance of the doctrine of the resurrection. Paul explains that Christ as the last Adam was the first person in history to be resurrected from the dead, the first of others who will be resurrected from the dead (15:20). Then Paul compares the two Adams in 15:21: "For as by a man came death, by a man has come also the resurrection of the dead." In other words, the first Adam failed in his task and brought death with him in the wake of his disobedience and failure. In contradistinction, the last Adam accomplished his task and brought with him life, eternal resurrection life in the wake of his obedience and accomplishment. Christ as the last Adam is reigning now by virtue of his resurrection. The first Adam was destined to rule the world to come (Heb 2:5–8). If Adam completed his royal task of dominion, the first Adam would have consummated his purpose in glorifying God. Afterwards he would have been enthroned with God in glory. In contrast, Christ did in fact attain Adam's original destiny and now has attained dominion in the world to come. Unlike the first Adam, the last Adam entered that imperishable kingdom that the first Adam failed to do.

In Hebrews 2, Paul's teaching of the last Adam is echoed. The human race was destined to rule this world and the world to come, but is not remotely close to ruling this world, much less the world to come. In contrast, everything is not subject to the human race; because of the first Adam (Heb 2:8), ". . . we see [the last Adam] who for a little while was made lower than the angels, namely Jesus, crowned with glory and honor" (2:9). The first Adam was a failure, whereas the second Adam was a success, attaining the goal first offered to the first Adam. VanDrunen says Hebrews 2:9 teaches us four truths to ponder or reflect upon. First, by virtue of the incarnation, Christ Jesus stepped into the first Adam's position. Second, Jesus suffered a lifetime of grief, misery, and woe that ended at the cross while all along remaining perfectly obedient. Third, as a faithful priest he offered up his obedience unto suffering and death as an offering to the Father. In turn, the last Adam attained the original Adamic destiny in the world to come, now crowned with glory and honor. Fourth, the last Adam did all of this vicariously for everyone who put their trust in him.[151] VanDrunen correctly notes that these four themes recur throughout the book of Hebrews. He says,

> Unlike the first Adam, who failed to finish the task be began, Jesus completed his work perfectly, being "without sin" (4:15). In

151. VanDrunen, *Living in God's Two Kingdoms*, 54–55.

contrast to the first Adam, he conquered Satan (2:4). Through this work he became qualified as a perfect high priest "after the order of Melchizedek" (5:10; 7:1–28). The first Adam was to exercise dominion as a king (Genesis 1:26–28) and guard the garden as a royal priest (Genesis 2:15), thus Jesus became the perfect Priest-King, like Melchizedek who was "king of Salem, priest of the Most High of God" (Hebrews 7:1). Whereas the first Adam allowed God's original temple to be polluted and caused human being to be expelled from his presence, Jesus has cleansed the holy place and won re-entry into God's presence—not simply in an earthly sanctuary but a heavenly sanctuary (9:11–28). Jesus achieved the original destiny, "the world to come" (2:5). He "entered God's rest" when he "passed through the heavens" (4:10, 14), so that he is now "exalted above the heavens" (7:26) and "seated at the right hand of the throne of the Majesty in heaven, a minister in the holy places, in the true tent that the Lord set up . . ." (8:1–2). Having finished his work in this world, he "Sat down at the right hand of God" (10:12. The great Priest and Kind has entered the world-to-come.[152]

Believers' Share In Christ's Accomplishment

This is how Christ, the last Adam, accomplished the original task of the first Adam as demonstrated in Scripture. But how do believers share in the glory of world to come? Paul and the author of Hebrews are explicit that God treats believers as though they have perfectly completed the original task assigned to Adam, but accomplished by Christ. Not only are our sins forgiven, but believers are declared, credited, or imputed righteous and obedient in God's sight by way of Christ's accomplishment, that is, justified by grace through faith in Christ's passive and active obedience. Also, Christ attained the destiny once held out to Adam, the destiny of dominion in the world to come. What is clearly evinced in Scripture is that believers presently participate in Christ's dominion not only in this world (see Rev 1:9) but also in the world to come. In Ephesians 2:4–7, Paul clearly teaches that in Christ believers are "made . . . alive together in Christ . . . and raised . . . up with him and [has] seated us with him in the heavenly places in Christ Jesus." Paul teaches in 2 Corinthians 5:17 that believers in Christ are already "new creations." Paul is saying that we can currently claim the rights and privileges and obligations of the world to come. Though believers are

152. VanDrunen, *Living in God's Two Kingdoms*, 55–56.

Kingdom Theology

residents of this world, we are currently citizens of the heavenly kingdom, where Christ rules and reigns in the age to come. As VanDrunen says,

> Thus the Christian life should not follow the pattern that the first Adam was supposed to follow. Christians are not to pursue righteous obedience in this world and then, as a consequence, enter the world-to-come. Instead, Christians have been made citizens of the world-to-come by a free gift of grace and now, as a consequence, are to live righteous and obedient lives in this world.[153]

In Hebrews 2:9–10, not only is Jesus spoken of as already having acquired or attained the original destiny, as one who has been crowned with "glory and honor," but believers are too by virtue of his accomplishment "bringing many sons to glory." Jesus leads his children to glory in the wake of his accomplishment of the dominion/cultural mandate. In Hebrews 4:4, Jesus has "passed through the heavens." In the wake of this, "there remains a Sabbath rest for the people of God" (4:9).

The Sabbath rest awaits for believers in glory when we are glorified in our bodies by means of the resurrection. But this consummate state of glory is "already" possessed by believer in part. Case in point is Romans 8:29–30:

> For those whom he foreknew he also predestined to be conformed to the image of his Son, in order that he might be the firstborn among many brothers. And those whom he predestined he also called, and those whom he called he also justified, and those whom he justified he also glorified.

The majority report by most evangelicals is that this classic text regarding the "golden chain of redemption" is held up, in the order of salvation, as a future hope in the age to come, the consummation realized in the believer's future by means of the resurrection.[154] The obvious problem with interpreting ἐδόξασεν as future is that the verb is in the aorist tense. Daniel Wallace goes so far to say this verb is in the "future aorist" tense. [155] Ortlund argues otherwise. He contends that Paul intends to say exactly what the aorist tense of the verb means to convey: the past tense.[156] The lens or "macro-historical

---

153. VanDrunen, *Living in God's Two Kingdoms*, 56–57.

154. Even Beale, who is one of the prominent proponents of inaugurated eschatology, takes the position that Rom 8:30 is speaking about future glorification via the future bodily resurrection. See Beale, *New Testament Biblical Theology*, 501, 503.

155. Wallace, *Greek Grammar*, 563–64.

156. Ortlund, "Inaugurated Glorification," 132. Ortlund argues that the verb is an

framework" against which he reads Romans 8:29–30, and Paul in general, is inaugurated eschatology. By inaugurated eschatology he means "all the hopes and dreams and promises of the OT, which Jews expected to happen on the final day at the end of history, have begun in the middle of history, in Christ."[157] Ortlund argues convincingly for a consistent eschatology where glorification will not only take place at the end of history but has already taken place back during the middle of history in Christ. That is to say, those who are in Christ have already experienced glorification in part; the glory that man lost due to Adam's transgression has been reinstated in Christ, the second and last Adam. The divine image, manifest supremely in Christ, has been restored. Bavinck strongly suggests this as well:

> Although [glorification] is treated only at the conclusion of dogmatics, in the doctrine of the last things, it nevertheless actually belongs to the way of salvation (via salutis).... In Romans 8:30, the apostle lists three benefits in which God's foreknowledge is realized, namely, calling, justification, and glorification. All these benefits are temporal. Similarly, the phrase "he glorified" (ἐδόξασεν) does not refer— at least not exclusively and in the first place –to the glorification that awaits believers after death or after the day of judgment but, as is evident from the aorist, to the glorification that believers, by the renewal of the Holy Spirit, already experienced on earth and that is fully unfolded at their resurrection on the last day[158]

CONCLUSION

Since the inauguration of the kingdom of God's new creation is an "already" current reality in this present age, and the consummation of the kingdom of God's new creation is a "not yet" future inevitability for the age to come— both being a work of God and God alone, which has been demonstrated—then the message (that is, the gospel) of the inauguration of the kingdom of God's new creation is something God's people in their mission are mandated to witness, proclaim, and pronounce to the world. As has been demonstrated, the mission of God's people is very narrow and specific. The reason why the mandate of the Great Commission is narrow

---

ingress aorist, "indicating the beginning of a process that will one day be completed.... [with the accent on] a single event in two phases."

157. Ortlund, "Inaugurated Glorification," 114.
158. Bavinck, *Reformed Dogmatics*, 3:594.

and specific is due to the implication of the inauguration of the kingdom of God's new creation. The kingdom of God's new creation has been reinstated in Christ. Christ has fully accomplished all that Adam failed to do. What Adam failed to do—that is, to perfectly obey the cultural mandate to glorify God in his capacity to achieve dominion in this world and the world to come—the second and last Adam has accomplished. Christ has attained man's original destiny on behalf of those whom are in Christ. The last Adam perfectly accomplished the task originally given to the first Adam. Jesus, in his life, death, resurrection, and ascension, crushed the head of Satan as the righteous priest and king in this world, attaining the destiny—that is, entering into glory in the world to come—that Adam failed to do. Christ as the last Adam is reigning now by virtue of His resurrection. The first Adam was destined to rule the world to come (Heb 2:5–8). By completing his royal task of dominion, the first Adam was to image the glory of God. Subsequently, he was to be enthroned with God in glory. In contrast, Christ attained Adam's original destiny and has now attained dominion in the world to come. Unlike the first Adam, the last Adam entered that imperishable kingdom that the first Adam failed to do. In light of this second Adamic state accomplished by Christ Jesus, this Adamic state is imputed to believers. Believers, who are united with Christ, claim the victory of Christ as their own and are "already" citizens of the world to come, though "not yet" residents until Christ comes to consummate his kingdom. This glory that believers share with Christ is not a superficial triumphalism. Our present glory is hidden in weakness as we faithfully endure tribulation. The reason why the mandate of the Great Commission is restricted in nature is because Christ has perfectly accomplished the first mandate of the original Adamic Commission. By obeying the mandate, the church neither substantively adds to Christ's accomplishment nor substantively builds the kingdom. She inherits what Christ has accomplished as coheirs. This is why the mandate of the Great Commission given to the church consists of proclaiming and preaching what Christ, and Christ alone, has definitely accomplished; that is, preaching the gospel message of the inaugurated, new-creational kingdom of God (evangelism) and teaching this kingdom message of obedience and submission to the king. The church is to testify and bear witness to the present rule of Christ to the nations irrespective of race or ethnicity. In short, the church's mandate is restricted to those actions and ministries taken on by the church to present, to witness, and to proclaim the gospel message of the kingdom of God's new creation to the unregenerate. As

Practical Implications

Psalm 2:12 says, our message is a mandate, a mandate and warning to "Kiss the Son, lest he be angry, and you perish in the way, for his wrath is quickly kindled. Blessed are all who take refuge in him." Our mandate is to relay this message of amnesty, that is, the gracious and merciful terms of surrender of our conquering King to an already conquered enemy. It was customary in the ancient Near East before kings razed and conquered lands—i.e., demolished walls, public buildings, infrastructure, etc.—to first expend much effort through the power of persuasion to convince foreign people to submit willingly. The mandate of the Great Commission is simply King Jesus sending his ambassadors to relay the message that the King of the age to come has already conquered the god of this age, that total eschatological judgment and destruction are impending. Holy Spirit power has been given to the church to persuade the foreign nations to submit willingly in this dispensation of grace and mercy.[159]

---

159. See Dalley, "Ancient Mesopotamian Military Organization," 420.

CHAPTER 4

Summary, Conclusion, and Reflections Summary

In conclusion, both the kingdom of God, in general, and the inaugurated eschatological rule of God's new-creational kingdom, in particular, have an effect on the nature and perspective of missions. The effect is that the nature of the mission of the church is curtailed. Since the inauguration of the kingdom of God's new creation is an "already" current reality in this present age, and the consummation of the kingdom of God's new creation is a "not yet" future inevitability for the age to come—both being a work of God and God alone, which has been demonstrated—then the message (that is, the gospel) of the inauguration of the kingdom of God's new creation is something the mission of God's people are mandated to witness, proclaim, and pronounce to the world. As demonstrated, the mission of God's people as a church is very narrow and specific. The reason why the mandate of the Great Commission is narrow and specific is due to the implication of the inauguration of the kingdom of God's new creation. The kingdom of God's new creation has been reinstated in Christ. Christ has fully accomplished all that Adam failed to do. What Adam failed to do as king—that is, to perfectly obey the cultural mandate to glorify God in his capacity to achieve dominion in this world and the world to come—the second and last Adamic king has accomplished. Christ has attained man's original destiny on behalf of those who are in Christ. The last Adamic king perfectly accomplished the task originally given to the first Adamic king. In Jesus' life, death, resurrection, and ascension, he crushed the head of Satan as the righteous priest and king in this world, attaining the destiny—that is, entering into glory in the world to come—that the first Adamic king failed to do. Christ as the last Adamic king is reigning now by virtue of his resurrection. The first Adamic king was destined to rule the world to come (Heb 2:5–8). By completing his royal task of dominion, the first Adamic king was to image the glory of God. Afterwards he was to be enthroned with God in glory. In contrast, Christ attained Adam's original destiny and now has attained dominion in the world to come. Unlike the first Adamic king, the last Adamic king entered that imperishable kingdom that the first Adamic king failed to do. In light of this second Adamic state accomplished by Christ Jesus, this Adamic state is imputed to believers. Believers, who are united with Christ, claim the victory of Christ as their own and are "already" citizens of the world to come, though "not yet" residence until Christ comes to consummate his kingdom. This glory that believers share with Christ is not a superficial triumphalism. As I noted above, our present victory or glory is hidden in weakness as we faithfully endure tribulation (Rev 1:9). The reason why the mandate of the Great Commission is restricted in nature is because Christ has perfectly accomplished the first mandate of the original Adamic Commission. By obeying the mandate, the church neither adds to Christ's accomplishment, nor does she build the kingdom that Christ has inaugurated. She in large part inherits what Christ has accomplished as coheirs. This is why the mandate of the Great Commission given to the church consists of proclaiming and preaching what Christ, and Christ alone, has definitively accomplished, that is, to preach the gospel message of the inaugurated, new-creational kingdom of God (Word, sacrament, and evangelism) and to teach this kingdom message of obedience and submission (discipline) to the king. The church is to testify and bear witness to the present rule of Christ to the nations (disciple the nations) irrespective of race or ethnicity. In short, the church's mandate is restricted to those actions and ministries taken on by the church to present, to witness, and to proclaim the gospel message of the kingdom of God's new creation to the unregenerate. As Psalm 2:12 says, our message is a mandate, a mandate and warning to "Kiss the Son, lest he be angry, and you perish in the way, for his wrath is quickly kindled. Blessed are all who take refuge in him." Our mandate is to relay this message, that is, the terms of surrender, of our conquering king to an already conquered enemy, that many will submit to Christ as their king as the kingdom of grace expands in this age by means of discipling the nations, that is, leaving their old way of life and participating in the expanding nature of the original commission in Genesis now transposed in the mandate of the Great Commission; the church participates in ruling and subduing by spiritually overcoming the influence of evil in the heart of unregenerate humanity, who are rebelling against Christ's kingdom, by making disciples, that is, evangelism and teaching and living out one's obedience to the Word of God.[1]

REFLECTIONS

My project has been about the church as an institution in relation to missions. Before I elaborate on my reflection of the church as an institution, first let me say a bit more about the narrow focus of my thesis. I have attempted to demonstrate that the Great Commission is inherently narrow. However, this is not to say there is not a positive side to my thesis. What is it we gain from recapturing a narrow focus? On the positive side, Christ has not only given his church a narrow agenda, but has also given us a strategic plan to fulfill that agenda. What is this strategic plan? How are we to fulfill both mandates? First, we must utilize the methods of making disciples. Second, we must exercise dominion in light of both the Great Commandment and Great Commission.

First, concerning the former, we must utilize the methods of making disciples. What are these methods? In the Reformed tradition these methods are preaching, teaching, and the sacraments—all being means of grace. This is an important distinction. Methods as a means of works reduce missions to the pragmatic techniques of men. Methods as a means of grace underscores that God is the one at work, that is, "God's act of raising us from spiritual death by the word of the gospel and ratifying publicly his covenant pledge through baptism and the Supper."[2] It's God who gives and we receive. On the basis of the Great Commission, the Reformers affirmed the marks of the visible, local church; that is, Word and sacraments and church discipline. Christ has promised to be present with us to the "end of the age" (Matt 28:20) in the authoritative context of preaching, teaching,

---

1. Beale, *New Testament Biblical Theology*, 53. Beale says, "Hence, the 'ruling and subduing' of Genesis 1:28 now includes spiritually overcoming the influence of evil in the hearts of unregenerate humanity that has multiplied upon earth. The implication is that the notion of physical newborn children "increasing and multiplying" in the original Genesis 1:28 commission now includes people who have left their old way of life and have become spiritually newborn and have come to reflect the image of God's glorious presence and participate in the expanding nature of the Genesis 1:26–28 commission."

2. Horton, *Gospel Commission*, 165.

Summary, Conclusion, And Reflections Summary

and church discipline through the ministry of the keys, that is, binding (retaining) and loosing (forgiving) sins (Matt 16:19; 18:15–20). In preaching and teaching we receive more than knowledge of Christ; we receive a superabundance of Christ's enabling grace, that is, "grace upon grace" (John 1:16). The Word of God is active in the hearts of believers, mortifying hearts through the law and vivifying hearts through the gospel; it's active and living, judging and justifying (Heb 4:12–14). Preaching and teaching are more than about knowledge on how to get saved, but the very means by which men are saved (Rom 10:17). Preaching is a "word from God, through an authorized messenger, unlocking prison doors . . . a strange voice from heaven through a sinner like us."[3] The same is true for the sacraments; that is, God acts. As a means of grace, baptism is God's claim on us. God pledges to commit himself to us. This is the same for the Lord's Supper; as a means of grace, believers are united with Christ and his atoning death through the Supper (1 Cor 10:18–22). The mandate of the Great Commission is not only a mandate, but God's means of grace, a grace that gives us faith in Christ and enables us to endure and flourish to the end of our lives and this age. In short, we gain Christ as opposed to losing sight of Christ by employing the pragmatic techniques of men; that is, climbing the ladder to heaven through various spiritual techniques and exercises. TED Talks, video clips, liturgical dance, stage props, icons, rosary beads—these mission creep means to a mission creep end gain nothing, at the expense of losing Christ's enabling grace upon grace.

Second, we must not only utilize the methods of making disciples, but we must exercise dominion in light of the Great Commission. As noted above, Christ has restored our functional image-bearing capacity for godly dominion. It's not fully restored, but is being restored by means of sanctification. First, in part, what this means is that man can pursue his cultural pursuits of dominion for the glory of God in light of the Great Commandment under the covenant of common grace. Fallen man, in Adam, in his cultural pursuits defrauds God of his glory in seeking human glory, that is, vainglory. But redeemed man in Christ can pursue his/her cultural pursuits by means of his/her vocation and bring glory to God. The difference is not based on the objective nature of our cultural artifacts; a Christian surgeon and a pagan doing surgery are fundamentally doing the same thing, that is, loving their neighbor by means of restoring health.[4] However, the differ-

---

3. Horton, *Gospel Commission*, 167.
4. This is not to deny that modern science and medicine are products of a Christian

ence is based on the subjective nature or the motive for engaging cultural activities. The former is for vainglory; the latter is for the glory of God and true love of neighbor.

Second, in part, what this also means is that redeemed men can pursue godly dominion. Just as Jesus as king has received a kingdom to exercise dominion, likewise we, his disciples, have also received his kingdom (Luke 22:29–30). Just as Christ exercised dominion in his kingdom, likewise disciples are to exercise dominion in light of the Great Commission. But this exercise of dominion is not an earthly dominion, but heavenly dominion. Poythress says that this "... heavenly dominion has already been achieved for us and into which we have already entered in union with Christ (Ephesians 2:6). We think of dominating non-Christians politically and economically rather than praying for Christ to dominate them through renewing their hearts."[5]

The original mandate to be "fruitful and multiply" has been transposed into "go make disciples of the nations." By making disciples of the nations, the church is participating in godly dominion. How? In Isaiah 9:6–7, the prophet notes that Christ's kingdom/government will increase. Christ's kingdom will not arrive all at once in consummative form. Christ has definitively inaugurated his kingdom and will definitively consummate his kingdom. When Christ ascended, his spiritual kingdom here on earth was to advance. In Hebrews 10:13–14, the author says that "Since that time he awaits for his enemies to be made his footstool, because by one sacrifice he has made perfect forever those who are being made holy." Jesus is reigning in heaven, and here on earth his spiritual kingdom of grace is progressively conquering by making a footstool out of his enemies. This is accomplished by his sacrifice on the cross by turning enemies into friends. And this is applied by the Holy Spirit through the church's ministry of the Word to evangelize. The kingdom of grace on earth is expanding as a spiritual battle or spiritual holy war takes place, a battle for dominion over hearts and minds and souls, as the lost, guilt-ridden, self-destructive generations of men are reconciled to God. In short, discipleship is the means of godly

---

worldview; that the Christian faith has put a distinct imprint on medicine, in particular, and culture at large. But ancient pagans employed and practiced medicine well before the Christian faith. Even though culture is common, it's not uniform.

5. Poythress, *Shadows of Christ*, 358. Poythress correctly observes that this "heavenly dominion" is the correct application of the Old Covenant holy war paradigm transposed to fit the new-creational reality in light of Christ's dominion. For example, see Poythress, *Shadows of Christ*, 139–53.

Summary, Conclusion, And Reflections Summary

dominion, of being fruitful and multiplying, of disciplining the nations. As noted above, the church is to testify and bear witness to the present the rule of Christ to the nations irrespective of race or ethnicity. The church's mandate is to present, to witness, and to proclaim the gospel message of the kingdom of God's new creation to the unregenerate. As Psalm 2:12 says, our message is a mandate, a mandate and warning to "Kiss the Son, lest he be angry, and you perish in the way, for his wrath is quickly kindled. Blessed are all who take refuge in him." Our mandate is to relay this message of amnesty, that is, the terms of surrender, of our conquering king to an already conquered enemy.

Last but not least, there is another sense in which redeemed man can (and ought to) pursue godly dominion. As noted above, in light of the second Adamic state accomplished by Christ Jesus, this Adamic state is imputed to believers. Believers, who are united with Christ, claim the victory of Christ as their own and are "already" citizens of the world to come, though "not yet" residents until Christ comes to consummate his kingdom. This glory that believers share with Christ is not only imputed, but is an actual possession and participation of dominion. But it's not a "superficial triumphalism."[6] Our present glory is hidden in weakness as we faithfully endure tribulation. The "ironic pattern of redemptive victory" and dominion describes how we as believers in this age exercise dominion and victory. As noted in my third chapter, in Revelation 1:9 John acknowledges

---

6. I call it "superficial" because whatever social or cultural triumph the church has over and in this age is provisional and temporal and reversible at best. The inauguration and expansion (i.e., the expansion of grace in the heart of God's elect) and consummation of the kingdom of God are irreversible conditions because they cannot be frustrated and impeded by sin. As a general equity theonomist (i.e., a confessional theonomist), I consider Calvin's Geneva as an example of triumph, one I believe in part is a model for Christian ethics and a social vision for society, minus its theocratic notion of magistrates. However, such triumphs are short-lived; with the ebb and flow of history, triumphs and declensions are inherent cycles and patterns of this age. The triumph we are looking for as Christians will be at the end of the age, when Christ consummates his kingdom. Until then said triumphs are superficial and do not and cannot advance the kingdom of God's new-creational reign. It's a categorical mistake to equate or connect cultural triumphalism in this age with the eschatological triumphalism of the new-creational kingdom in the age to come. The former will never bring about the latter. We must never blur the lines. Also, we must first reorient the church and her mission according to the gospel of the kingdom of God's new-creational reign under the covenant of redemptive grace before we (i.e., in our Christian vocations) can repair our degenerate society according to God's moral law under the covenant of common grace, that is, the common grace of God's providential, protological kingdom that is preserving this age until the day of the Lord. See Clowney, "Politics of the Kingdom."

this tension; that is, saints, while being members in the kingdom of God, are also partners, partners who are patiently enduring tribulation. Patiently enduring tribulation is the present mode of dominion and victory in this present age.

Back to my reflection of the church as an institution, my project has been about the church as an institution in relation to missions. As an institution, the church is governed by God's gift of ordained officers—that is, pastors (teaching elders), elders, and deacons—who are commissioned to plant churches, proclaim the Word, administer the sacraments, and exercise spiritual discipline. These officers of the church are most responsible for the work of the Great Commission because they are officers of the institutional church. The keys of the kingdom are handed to the collective officers of the church, not to individual Christians. There is a distinction between the church and a Christian's individual vocation. As Horton says,

> Christians are called to do many things that the church is not called to do. The place where believers are *made* salt and light is wherever the Word is preached and the sacraments are administered, but the primary place where believers *are* salt and light is the world. Some believers are called to offices in the church, but most are called to offices in the world.[7]

Many Christian offices in the world may call Christians to work closely with the church. Publishing houses, schools, seminaries, voluntary organizations, etc.—these parachurch organizations can meet needs and challenges that the church may not be as competent or as efficient to do alone to further the gospel.[8] However, there are other such voluntary organizations where the church is not competent to do such work. Case in point is the humanitarian aid provided by hospital ships. Hospital ships provide a variety of humanitarian aid. The church is neither commissioned nor competent to operate hospital ships to provide such a variety of humanitarian aid. The converse is true for some parachurch organizations: some may be

---

7. Horton, *Gospel Commission*, 209.

8. Some examples are seminaries like Reformed Presbyterian Theological Seminary and publishing companies like Crown and Covenant. Boards of foreign and domestic missions, Christian boards of education and publication, and Christian schools, etc.—these are much-needed and efficient means to further the mission of the church in collaboration with and under the auspices and oversight of the church.

Summary, Conclusion, And Reflections Summary

competent but not commissioned to fulfill the mandate of the Great Commission. Others are commissioned and capable.⁹

This is an important distinction to keep in mind, especially when discussing the distinction between the mandate of the Great Commission and the Second Great Commandment. When it comes to the Great Commandment, most individual Christians in light of the myriad of gifts and offices are called to the offices in the world in various vocations. In fact most of all the material needs in the world are met by the unregenerate and regenerate joining forces (in social action to love one's neighbor) either as cobelligerents against common enemies—for example, such as Roe v. Wade, sex trafficking, drug abuse, etc.—or as collaborators for a common cause—for example, in curing cancer, ameliorating standards of living, alleviating hunger, etc.¹⁰ Every day, your average Christian works together with non-Christians in the context of common grace activities for the common, temporal good. This is all in light of the Great Commandment under the administration of the covenant of common grace instituted in a postdiluvian world to preserve this world/age, not to redeem this world/age. This is because, as noted, common grace preserves nature; redeeming grace consummates nature.¹¹

---

9. Case in point is Ravi Zacharias and his ministry, Ravi Zacharias International Ministries (RZIM). RZIM was a parachurch ministry very capable and competent in fulfilling the Great Commission, but was not commissioned because there was no ecclesiastical judicatory that exercised jurisdiction and oversight, no church board to hold Zacharias and the ministry accountable.

10. This is another example of dominion, in the sense that when both the regenerate and unregenerate join said forces, they are in fact engaged in a penultimate, protological notion of dominion under the Noahic covenant of common grace.

11. I do believe that grace can restore nature in the vein of Bavinck, contrary to some Reformed/radical two-kingdoms proponents like VanDrunen and Horton. Case in point is 1 Cor 7:14. In Paul's context he was dealing with mixed marriages. Some believers were concerned that their unbelieving spouses would defile them and their marriages. As the saying goes, a bad apple spoils the batch. But, Paul says, it's the exact opposite: instead of a Christian being defiled and made unholy by their unbelieving spouse, the unbelieving spouse is made holy by the Christian spouse. This doesn't mean that an unbelieving spouse will automatically be saved, but it also doesn't mean that there is not a sanctifying influence, a sort of spillover of "covenant grace" on those in a Christian household, those close to a Christian. For example: Joseph in Potiphar's house; Abraham's pleading with God in Gen 18:16–33; 39:5. This trumps living in a totally pagan home, decaying because of sin. Unbelieving husbands should thank God for their Christian wives! Unbelieving wives should thank God for their Christian husbands! Unbelieving children should thank God for their Christian parents who drag them to church every Sunday! This is what Paul means by "Otherwise your children would be unclean, but as it is, they are holy." Calvin

In contrast, some Christians are called to offices in the church that also address material, temporal needs in light of the Great Commission vis-à-vis the Great Commandment. The care of material, temporal needs is constitutive of the Great Commission too because mercy ministries are taught in Scripture, which is a commandment from our Lord to be obeyed. Christ called his apostles to care for the souls of saints. The office of the deaconate was instituted to care for the bodies of saints. The institution of the deaconate is described in Acts 6:1–4. The spiritual needs of believers were met by the apostles (including elders), while temporal needs of believers were met by the deacons. Later a separate office of deacon was established to care for the material needs of believers.

One clear example of the importance of caring for the material needs of believers is the collection that the apostle Paul took up for the Jewish saints in Jerusalem in 1 Corinthians 16.

Paul says that this collection is to be taken up for saints. In context, the term "saints" mean the poor saints in Jerusalem, that is, the poor Jewish Christians in Jerusalem. Paul had taken upon himself to spearhead a fundraiser for Jewish Christians in Jerusalem. This collection is specified in a number of places in the New Testament, for example, in 2 Corinthians 8:1–7:

> We want you to know, brothers, about the grace of God that has been given among the churches of Macedonia, ² for in a severe test of affliction, their abundance of joy and their extreme poverty have overflowed in a wealth of generosity on their part. ³ For they gave

---

calls this an "exclusive privilege" via proximity to the church. The salt of grace is preserving the home. Grace does restore common grace institutions, restore them so as to preserve nature. But this restoration is not redemptive, redemptive in an eschatological, new-creational sense because the family is not a new creation destined for new creation. The same goes for Christian doctors, Christian magistrates, Christian lawyers, Christian teachers, Christian financial advisors, Christian composers, etc.—these Christian vocations/offices in the world put a distinct stamp (e.g., J. S. Bach) on our world and culture, but not a new-creational stamp. Converted Christians are citizens of the nations they inhabit. And as citizens of nations we bear responsibility for the nations and commonwealths and political communities, bearing the responsibility to bear a distinct stamp on our culture as Christian citizens of the nations, but that stamp is not a new-creational stamp. William Wilberforce, formed and informed by his Christian faith, was a pivotal figure who helped bring an end to the transatlantic slave trade, bearing his responsibility for the nations based on his station in life. However, his stamp on the nations was not a new-creational stamp. Making disciples bears the stamp of new creation in the lives of God's elect as God's people are harvested, gathered, and perfected. For more on the notion of "covenant grace" see Kuiper, *Calvin on Common Grace*, 192–204.

Summary, Conclusion, And Reflections Summary

> according to their means, as I can testify, and beyond their means, of their own accord, ⁴ begging us earnestly for the favor of taking part in the relief of the saints— ⁵ and this, not as we expected, but they gave themselves first to the Lord and then by the will of God to us. ⁶ Accordingly, we urged Titus that as he had started, so he should complete among you *this act of grace.* ⁷ But as you excel in everything—in faith, in speech, in knowledge, in all earnestness, and in our love for you—see that you excel in this act of grace also.

Also, Paul says in Romans 15:25–26, "At present, however, I am going to Jerusalem bringing aid to the saints. For Macedonia and Achaia have been pleased to make some contribution for the poor among the saints at Jerusalem." And he says in Acts 24:17, "Now after several years I came to bring alms to my nation and to present offerings." So it's clear from Scripture that Paul was spearheading a fundraiser to raise money for poor Jewish Christian in Jerusalem. Why was Paul fundraising? Paul was fundraising for two reasons. The first reason was economic. In the ancient world, there was no such thing as a social safety net. Unlike in modern times in the West, there was no government welfare system. But there were charities and associations that provided for the poor. A case in point were the *eranoi*. These associations banded together to provide interest-free loans for the poor, people trapped in a disaster and who couldn't meet their needs. They would pay back these loans when they got back on their feet. There were also gifts given that did not need to be paid back. However, these loans and gifts were only for fellow Greeks. The Jews also had their associations that gave to the poor. Jews would give money to the local synagogue and earmark that money for poor relief. Poor Jews would apply for the relief to the leadership at the synagogue based on need. The synagogue would vet their request and, based on the need, give to meet that need. Here's the issue: Greeks only gave to fellow Greeks; Jews in Jerusalem only gave to Jews who were members of the synagogue. If you were a member in good standing, you were eligible for poor relief. However, if you were not in good standing—for example, you were excommunicated from the synagogue—you were not eligible for said funds. What offense would put someone out of the synagogue, making him disqualified for poor relief? John 9:22 gives an example of such an offense: "His parents said these things because they feared the Jews, for the Jews had agreed already that if anyone confessed that He was Christ, he would be put out of the synagogue." This means Jewish Christians suffered the most due to poverty. This is why in the early days of the church saints took care of other poor saints. Luke describes the very early days of the church in Acts 2:42–47:

> And they devoted themselves to the apostles' teaching and the fellowship, to the breaking of bread and the prayers. And awe came upon every soul, and many wonders and signs were being done through the apostles. And all who believed were together and had all things in common. And they were selling their possessions and belongings and distributing the proceeds to all, as any had need. And day by day, attending the temple together and breaking bread in their homes, they received their food with glad and generous hearts, praising God and having favor with all the people. And the Lord added to their number day by day those who were being saved.

If Greeks and Jews would take care of their own, then does it not make sense that we Christians would also take care of our own? This is one of the reasons why the church gave: it gave to take care of the economic needs of poor brothers and sisters because if they didn't do it, it would not be done. Also, the economic need for Jewish Christians in Jerusalem was even more critical because Jewish Christians were the poorest of Christians. Why? There were a number of reasons. First, Jerusalem (by the time of Christ and the apostles) was a very poor city in general. Jerusalem was poor for historical reasons (constant wars and conquests) and overpopulated; the resources would not keep up with the influx of Jewish immigration for religious reasons and repatriation. This drained the scarce resources of the city. Second was the problem of persecution. Jewish Christians were persecuted for their faith; poor Jewish Christians were excluded from the synagogue relief funds, and well-off Jews were excluded from making a living because their land and resources were confiscated. Third, wealthy Jewish Christians were running out of resources to give. If you have property and you are selling property to match the need(s) of your fellow Jewish Christians, then eventually you are going to run out of property to donate. These were the economic reasons why Paul was taking up a collection so as to assuage and ease Jewish Christian poverty in Jerusalem.

In summary, the first reason why the church gave was to take care of the economic needs of poor Jewish Christians in Jerusalem. But there is a second reason: the second reason is Christian unity! Jesus said this in John 17:20–23:

Summary, Conclusion, And Reflections Summary

> I do not pray for these alone, but also for those who will believe in Me through their word; that they all may be one, as You, Father, are in Me, and I in You; that they also may be one in Us, that the world may believe that You sent Me. And the glory which You gave Me I have given them, that they may be one just as We are one: I in them, and You in Me; that they may be made perfect in one, and that the world may know that You have sent Me, and have loved them as You have loved Me.

John 17 is the actual Lord's Prayer because Jesus is praying to God for all saints. What is Jesus praying for? He is praying for unity in the church. There are two related forms of unity: invisible unity and visible unity. Invisible unity is the unity we all have in Christ. This corresponds to the invisible church. This is what Jesus means in verse 21: "that they all may be one, as You, Father, are in Me, and I in You; that they also may be one in Us." However, Jesus also teaches another form of unity, a visible unity. Visible unity is the public display that manifests our invisible unity. This kind of unity is visible to the world; this unity is a witness to Christ and the invisible unity of the church. Our invisible unity (which is the indicative of faith) must be manifested in our actions. Here's the question: how do we manifest to the world that we are one in Christ? There are a number of options. First, there is institutional unity. The world can know that we are Christians by our organizational or denominational structures. The world can know we are Christians because we are Presbyterian. The world can know we are Christians because we are Methodist or Baptist or Assemblies of God, etc. Second, there is liturgical unity. Liturgical unity is how we worship. The world will know we are Christians for how we worship; for how we pray, for example, kneeling or not kneeling, holding hands high in the air or not holding hands high in the air. The world will know that we are one by how we preach; for example, lectionary preaching or topical preaching or expository preaching. The world will know that we are one by how we sing; for example, exclusive psalmody or hymnody, organ or piano, traditional or contemporary hymns. Just like institutional unity, I don't think this is the kind of unity that Jesus means. Third, there is unity of faith. This is not the subjective act of faith where you trust in Jesus Christ. That is invisible and inward. Only God knows whether the inward faith of someone is genuine or disingenuous. What I mean is a faith that manifests itself outwardly, what the Bible calls "the faith." This is the content of what we objectively confession with our mouths. We call this "doctrine"! The world will know we are one by our doctrine. Doctrine does distinguish true faith and religion from false faith and religion. How does the world know a Mormon from a Christian? Mormons do not believe in the transcendence and infinity of God, but all Christians do. Jehovah Witnesses do not believe in the deity of Christ, but all Christians do. Protestant liberalism does not believe in the penalsubstitutionary atonement of Christ or the virgin birth of Christ, but all Christians do. The peace and unity of the church is based on the purity of the church.

However, there is another form of unity, a fourth form: this is the unity of love. In fact, Jesus calls this fourth form of unity a "new commandment." Jesus says in John 13:34–35, "A new commandment I give to you, that you love one another; as I have loved you, that you also love one another. By this all will know that you are My disciples, if you have love for one another." The unity of love is visible unity, and this visible unity is the public display that manifests our invisible unity. This unity the world can see; this unity is a witness to Christ and the invisible unity of the church. Our invisible unity (which is the indicative of faith) must manifest itself in our charity (which is the imperative of love!) Here is Paul's point. The reason why Paul was collecting money to relieve the poverty of Jewish Christian is to unite the gentile church and the Jewish church. As we know, unity among gentile and Jewish Christians was a real problem in the early church. The Jerusalem church was Jewish. The churches in Asian Minor, Achaia, Macedonia, Galatian, Corinth, and Rome were gentile. Paul took a terrible situation (extreme poverty in Jerusalem) and not only relieved the economic needs of the Jerusalem church, but also relieving this need became an overwhelming, tangible, visible act of love. This collection from the gentile Christians in other parts of the world would go a long way to solidify and galvanize unity among gentile Christians and Jewish Christians. This one collection would kill two birds with one stone, solving two problems with one action.

In short, mercy ministry is a visible, tangible act of love where Christian discipleship takes place as the church cares for not only the spiritual needs, but the material needs of fellow Christians. However, the more difficult question that faces the church today is whether or not mercy ministry shoud be limited to fellow Christians or extended to unbelievers. There are a number of scriptures that some point to as evidence that the church is to extend mercy ministry (social action) to unbelievers. One such principal passage is Matthew 25:34–36. However, in verses 37 and 40 those in need are designated as "the least of these my brothers." It's clear from this principal passage that mercy ministries that attend to material needs are extended fellow believers not to unbelievers. In Galatians 6:10, Paul exhorts Christians to prioritize "doing good" to fellow believers (that is, "those who are of the household of faith") over unbelievers. But Paul is not clear whether he is calling Christians as officers of the church—officers who are obliged to care for the temporal good of believers— to extend that care to unbelievers as well, or merely exhorting individual Christians in light of the Great Commandment. I take it to be the latter because in my view, as I reflect, there is no exhortation in Scripture that obliges officers of the church to care for the temporal good of unbelievers as an element of the Great Commission. This does not mean that the church cannot do so. Earlier I noted that social action is not constitutive of the Great Commission, contrary to Stott, but this is not to say that social action cannot be a handmaiden to evangelism. Loving your neighbor (supplying physical needs) can be supportive of the gospel mission. If it supports, then it's wise for the church to invest in such a support. Case in point: Tenth Presbyterian Church in Philadelphia during the 1980s spearheaded a mercy ministry to AIDS victims. This medical ministry of attending to physical needs was employed to support evangelism (that is, attending to the greater spiritual needs of the soul).

As already noted, your everyday average Christian works together with non-Christians in the context of common grace activities for the common, temporal good—all in light of the Great Commandment under the administration of the covenant of common grace instituted in a postdiluvian world to preserve this world/age, not to redeem this world/age. But does this apply to the institution of the church? I see no evidence that Christians as officers of the church are obligated to care for the common, temporal good of unbelievers, in light of the mandate of the Great Commission under the administration of the covenant of special grace instituted by Christ our king. This is an important distinction. A Christian as Christian is different from a Christian as officer. The former operates in light of the Great Commandment under the administration of the covenant of common grace instituted to preserve this world/age. The latter operates in light of the Great Commission under the administration of the covenant of grace instituted to make disciples in this world/age.

I am not suggesting that the church cannot support relief efforts in the aftermath of a natural disaster or any other effort. Diaconal services could be extended to unbelievers. The church in her official capacity could extend such care and relief under the discretion of the board of deacons.

But the question is: *shall* or *ought* the church extend such care and relief? The same goes for, as I noted, the relationship between the handmaiden of social action in collaboration with evangelism. My contention is that the church is not obligated to engage in social action, though the church may prudently do so. In light of what Christ our king has accomplished, the Great Commission establishes a narrow mandate for the church in its official ministry. This is important to keep in mind. The church exercises immense spiritual authority, that is, ministerial power as she exercises the keys of the kingdom. The exercising of these keys is used to bind and loose consciences. This immense authority is based on the kingdom mandate of the Great Commission, a mandate that is very narrowly defined not only against mission creep, that is, the gradual shift of kingdom objectives, but also for conscience's sake. The church cannot bind the consciences of believers from either her pulpits or courts unless the church's directives are clearly grounded in the explicit mandate of the Great Commission or logically deduced from Scripture. The mission of the church is narrow (Matt 28:18–20) and the calling/ministry/vocation of individual believers is broad (Rom 12:1–2). If we fail to make this crucial distinction, the church's mission will lose its biblical emphasis on gospel proclamation through Word and sacrament, church planting (and strengthening), and discipleship. And if the church's mission is lost, then its authority structure, instantiated in the offices and officers of the church, devolves into illegitimacy, illegitimacy because the church is no longer advancing the kingdom ends by which she was mandated to do so by King Jesus. In short, if the institutional church fails to do this, we will be relinquishing and abdicating and abandoning our most singular and particular and peculiar kingdom of God vocation: that is, the harvesting and the gathering and the perfecting of the saints.

Bibliography

Alexander, T. Desmond. *From Eden to the New Jerusalem: Exploring God's Plan for Life on Earth*. Nottingham, UK: InterVarsity, 2008.
Allison, Dale C. *The End of the Ages Has Come*. Philadelphia: Fortress, 1985.
August, James. "The Messianic Hope of Genesis: The Protoevangelium and Patriarchal Promises." *Themelios* 42:1 (April 2017) 46–52.
Bailey, J. W. "The Temporary Messianic Reign in the Literature of Early Judaism." *Journal of Biblical Literature* 53:1 (1934) 170–87.
Baugh, S. M. *The Majesty on High: Introduction to the Kingdom of God in the New Testament*. CreateSpace, 2017.
Bavinck, Herman. *Reformed Dogmatics: Sin and Salvation in Christ*. Vol. 3. Translated by John Vriend. Grand Rapids: Baker, 2006.
Beale, G. K. *The Book of Revelation*. New International Commentary of the New Testament. Grand Rapids: Eerdmans, 1999.
———. "The Descent of the Eschatological Temple in the Form of the Spirit at Pentecost: Part 1: The Clearest Evidence." *Tyndale Bulletin* 56:1 (Spring 2005) 73–102.
———. "The Eschatological Conception of New Testament Theology." In *Eschatology in the Bible and Theology: Evangelical Essays at the Dawn of the New Millennium*, edited by Kent E. Brower and Mark W. Elliot, 11–52. Downer Grove, IL: InterVarsity, 1997.
———. *A New Testament Biblical Theology: The Unfolding of the Old Testament in the New*. Grand Rapids: Backer Academics, 2011.
———. *The Temple and the Church's Mission: A Biblical Theology of the Dwelling of God*. Downer Grove, IL: InterVarsity, 2014.
Beasley-Murray, George R. *Jesus and the Kingdom of God*. Grand Rapids: Eerdmans, 1986.
Behe, Michael J. *Darwin's Black Box: The Biochemical Challenge to Evolution*. New York: Free Press, 1996.
Bock, Darrell L., ed. *Three Views on the Millennium and Beyond*. Grand Rapids: Zondervan, 1999.
Boice, James. *The Gospel of Matthew: The Triumph of the King*. Vol. 2. Grand Rapids: Baker, 2006.
Bolt, John. "Just What Do You Mean—Kingdom of God?" *Calvin Theological Seminary* 51:2 (November 16: 259–82.
Bosch, David J. *Transforming Mission: Paradigm Shifts in Theology of Mission*. Maryknoll, NY: Orbis, 1991.
Brow, Robert. *Go Make Disciples: A New Model of Discipleship in the Church*. Wheaton, IL: Herald Shaw, 1981.

Bibliography

Brower, Kent E., and Mark W. Elliot, eds. *Eschatology in the Bible and Theology.* Downers Grove, IL: InterVarsity, 1997.
Bruce, F. F. "Age." In *The International Standard Bible Encyclopedia*, edited by G. W. Bromiley, vol. 1. Grand Rapids: Eerdmans, 1979.
Busenitz, Nathan. "The Kingdom of God and the Eternal State." *The Master's Seminary Journal* 23:2 (Fall 2012) 255–74.
Carson, D. A. *The Gospel According to John.* Grand Rapids: Eerdmans, 1991.
———. "Matthew." In *Expositor's Bible Commentary*, edited by F. E. Gaibelein, vol. 8. Grand Rapids: Zondervan, 1984.
———. "Partakers of the Age to Come." In *These Last Days: A Christian View of History*, edited by Richard D. Phillips and Gabriel N. E. Fluhrer. Phillipsburg: P&R, 2011.
Chalmers, Aaron. "The Importance of the Noahic Covenant in Biblical Theology." *Tyndale Bulletin* 60:2 (Fall 2009) 207–16.
Charles, R. H. *Eschatology, the Doctrine of a Future Life in Israel, Judaism, and Christianity: A Critical History.* New York: Schocken, 1963.
Chilton, Bruce. "The Kingdom of God in Recent Discussion." In *Studying the Historical Jesus: Evaluations of the State of Current Research*, edited by B. D. Chilton and C. A. Evans. NTTS 19. Leiden: Brill, 1994.
Cohn, Norman. *The Pursuit of the Millennium.* New York: Oxford University Press, 1970.
Cole, Alan. *The New Temple: A Study in the Origins of the Catechetical "Form" of the Church in the New Testament.* London: Tyndale, 1950.
Colson, Charles W. *Loving God.* Grand Rapids: Zondervan, 1983.
Clouse, Robert G., ed. *The Meaning of the Millennium: Four Views.* Downers Grove, IL: InterVarsity, 1977.
Clowney, Edmund. "The Final Temple." *Westminster Theological Journal* 35:2 (Winter 1973) 156–89.
———. "Politics of the Kingdom." *Westminster Theological Journal* 42:2 (Spring 1979) 291–310.
Cullman, Oscar. *Christ and Time.* Translated by Floyd V. Filson. Philadelphia: Westminster, 1950.
Dalley, Stephanie. "Ancient Mesopotamian Military Organization." In *Civilizations of the Ancient Near East*, edited by Jack M. Sasson, 1:413–22. Peabody, MA: Hendrickson, 2006, .
Danker, Frederick W., Walter Bauer, William F. Arndt, and F. Wilbur Gingrich. *A Greek-English Lexicon of the New Testament and Other Early Christian Literature.* 3rd ed. Chicago: University of Chicago Press, 2000.
Davies, W. D., and Dale C. Allison Jr. *A Critical and Exegetical Commentary on the Gospel According to Saint Matthew.* International Critical Commentary. Edinburgh: T. & T. Clark, 1988.
Davis, John Jefferson. *The Victor of Christ's Kingdom.* Moscow, ID: Canon, 1996.
DeYoung, Kevin, and Greg Gilbert. *What Is the Mission of the Church?: Making Sense of Social Justice, Shalom, and the Great Commission.* Wheaton, IL: Crossway, 2011.
Dillard, R. B. "Intrabiblical Exegesis and the Effusion of the Spirit in Joel." In *Creator, Redeemer, Consummator: A Festshrift for M. G. Kline*, edited by H. Griffith and J. R. Muether, 87–93. Greenville, SC: Reformed Academics, 2000.
Donaldson, Terence. *Jesus on the Mountain: A Study in Matthean Theology.* Journal for the study of the New Testament 8. Sheffield, UK: JSOT Press, 1985.

BIBLIOGRAPHY

Dunn, James D. G. *The Parting of the Ways between Christianity and Judaism and Their Significance for the Character of Christianity.* London: SCM, 1991.
Elliot, Mark. *The Survivors of Israel: A Reconsideration of the Theology of Pre-Christian Judaism.* Grand Rapids: Eerdmans, 2000.
Ellis, Peter F. *Matthew: His Mind and His Message.* Collegeville, MN: Liturgical, 1974.
Erickson, Millard J. *Contemporary Options in Eschatology: A Study of the Millennium.* 4th ed. Grand Rapids: Baker, 1992.
Evans, Craig, A. "Inaugurating the Kingdom of God and Defeating the Kingdom of Satan." *Bulletin for Biblical Research* 15:1 (2005) 49–75.
Ferdinando, Keith. "Mission: A Problem of Definition." *Themelios* 33:1 (May 2008) 46–59. http://thegospelcoalition.org/publications/33-1/mission-a-problem-of-definition.
Fesko, J. V. *Justification: Understanding the Classic Reformed Doctrine.* Phillipsburg, NJ: P&R, 2008.
Frame, John. *The Doctrine of the Knowledge of God.* Phillipsburg, NJ: P&R, 2006.
———. *The Escondido Theology: A Reformed Response to Two Kingdom Theology.* Lakeland, IL: Whitefield, 2010.
———. *Salvation Belongs to the Lord: An Introduction to System Theology.* Phillipsburg, NJ: P&R, 2006.
France, R. T. *The Gospel of Matthew.* New International Commentary on the New Testament. Grand Rapids: Eerdmans, 2007.
Gaffin, Richard, Jr. *The Centrality of the Resurrection of Christ.* Grand Rapids: Baker, 1978.
———. "Theonomy and Eschatology: Reflections on Postmillennialism." In *Theonomy: A Reformed Critique*, edited by William S. Barker and W. Robert Godfrey, 197–224. Grand Rapids: Zondervan, 1990.
Gage, Warren Austin. *The Gospel of Genesis: Studies in Protology and Eschatology.* Winona Lake, IN: Carpenter, 1954.
Gamble, Richard C. *The Whole Counsel of God: God's Final Revelation.* Vol. 2. Phillipsburg: P&R, 2018.
Gentry, Kenneth L., Jr. "Whose Victory in History?" In *Theonomy: An Informed Response*, edited by Gary North, 207–30. Tyler, TX: Institute for Christian Economics, 1991.
Gentry, Peter J., and Stephen J. Wellum. *Kingdom through Covenant: A Biblical-Theological Understanding of the Covenants.* Wheaten, IL: Crossway, 2012.
Gladd, Benjamin L., and Matthew S. Harmon. *Making All Things New: Inaugurated Eschatology for the Life of the Church.* Grand Rapids, : Baker Academic, 2016.
Goldstein, Warren S. "The Dialectics of Religious Conflict: Church-Sect, Denomination and the Culture Wars." *Culture and Religion* 12:1 (March 2011) 77–99.
Goerner, Henry C. "The Kingdom of God in America." *Review & Expositor* 35:2 (January 1938) 134–35.
Goldsworthy, Graeme. *Gospel and Kingdom: A Christian Interpretation of the Old Testament.* Waynesboro, GA: Paternoster, 2000.
Gray, John. *The Biblical Doctrine of the Reign of God.* Edinburgh: T. & T. Clark, 1979.
Green, William M. "The Christian View of History." *Restoration Quarterly* 1:3 (1957) 99-112.
Guthrie, George H. "Hebrews." In *Commentary on the New Testament of the Old Testament*, edited by G. K. Beale and D. A. Carson, 919–95. Grand Rapids: Baker Academic, 2007.
Hart, D. G., and John R. Muether. *Seeking a Better Country: 300 Years of American Presbyterianism.* Phillipsburg, NJ: P&R, 2007.

Bibliography

Hoekema, Anthony A. *The Bible and the Future*. Grand Rapids: Eerdmans, 1994.

———. *Created In God's Image*. Grand Rapids: Eerdmans, 1986.

Holwerda, David E. *Jesus and Israel*. Grand Rapids: Eerdmans, 1995.

Horton, Michael. *The Gospel Commission: Recovering God's Strategy for Making Disciples*. Grand Rapids: Baker, 2011.

Hunter, James. *To Change the World: The Irony, Tragedy, and Possibility of Christianity in the Late Modern World*. New York: Oxford University Press, 2010.

Irons, Charles Lee. "Meredith Kline's View of the Cultural Mandate." Paper presented to the Bahnsen Conference, hosted by Branch of Hope OPC in Torrance, CA, October 23, 2015. http://upper-register.com/papers/kline-cultural-mandate.pdf.

Johnson, DennisE. *Triumph of the Lamb*. Phillipsburg, NJ: P&R, 2001.

Kik, J. Marcellus. *The Eschatology of Victory*. Phillipsburg, NJ: P&R, 1971.

Kilner, John F. *Dignity and Destiny: Humanity in the Image of God*. Grand Rapids: Eerdmans, 2015.

Kim, Seyoon. *The Origin of Paul*. Grand Rapids: Eerdmans, 1982.

Kirk, Andrew. *The Good News of the Kingdom Coming*. Downer Grove, IL: InterVarsity, 1985.

Kline, Meredith G. *God, Heaven, and Har Magedon: A Covenantal Tale of Cosmos and Telos*. Eugene, OR: Wipf & Stock, 2006.

———. *Kingdom Prologue: Genesis Foundations for a Covenantal Worldview*. Eugene, OR: Wipf & Stock, 2006.

Kolawole, Oladotum Paul. "God's Image in Man: A Biblical Perspective." *Journal of Biblical Theology* 2:3 (July–September 2019) 37–49.

Köstenberger, J. Andreas. *The Mission of Jesus and the Disciples According to the Fourth Gospel: With Implications for the Fourth Gospel Purpose and the Mission of the Contemporary Church*. Grand Rapids: Eerdmans, 1998.

Kuiper, Herman. *Calvin on Common Grace*. Grand Rapids: Smitter, 1928.

Kuyper, Abraham. *Abraham Kuyper: A Centennial Reader*. Edited by James D. Bratt. Grand Rapids: Eerdmans, 1998.

———. *Common Grace: God's Gifts for a Fallen World*. Vol. 1. Edited by Jordan J. Ballor and Stephen J. Grabill, translated by Nelson D. Kloosterman and Ed M. Mass. Bellingham, WA: Lexham, 2016.

———. *Rooted and Grounded: The Church as Organism and Institution*. Grand Rapids: Christian's Library, 2013.

Ladd, George. *The Gospel of the Kingdom*. Grand Rapids: Eerdmans, 1959.

———. *Jesus and the Kingdom: The Eschatology of Biblical Realism*. New York: Harper & Row, 1964.

———. "Kingdom of God—Reign or Realm." *Journal of Biblical Literature* 81:3 (September 1961) 230–38.

———. *The Presence of the Future*. New York: Harper & Row, 1964.

———. *The Theology of the New Testament*. Grand Rapids: Eerdmans, 1974.

Levison, John R. "The Spirit and the Temple in Paul's Letter to the Corinthians." In *Paul and His Theology*, edited by Stanley Porter, 189–215. Leiden: Brill, 2006.

Longenecker, Richard N. *Paul, Apostle of Liberty: The Origin and Nature of Paul's Christianity*. Vancouver, BC: Regent College, 2003.

Marsh, John. *The Fullness of Time*. London: Nisbet, 1952.

Mathews, Kenneth A. *Genesis 1—11:26*. New American Commentary 1A. Nashville: B&H, 1996.

Bibliography

McCartney, Dan G. "Ecce Homo: The Coming of the Kingdom as the Restoration of Human Vicegerency." *Westminster Theological Journal* 56:1 (Spring 1994) 1–21.

McNeal, Reggie. *Missional Renaissance: Changing the Scorecard for the Church.* San Francisco: Jossey-Bass, 2009.

Middleton, J. Richard. *The Liberating Image: The Imago Dei in Genesis 1.* Grand Rapids: Brazos, 2005.

Moltmann, Jürgen. *Theology of Hope.* Translated by J. W. Leitch. New York: Harper & Row, 1967.

Moore, George Foot. *Judaism in the First Centuries of the Christian Era.* Vol. 1. Cambridge, MA: Harvard University Press, 1927.

Niebuhr, H. Richard. *Christ and Culture.* 3rd ed. New York: Harper Collins, 2001.

———. *The Kingdom of God in America.* New York: Harper Torchbook, 1959.

Niehaus, Jeffery. *God at Sinai.* Grand Rapids: Zondervan, 1995.

Nolland, John. *The Gospel of Matthew: A Commentary on the Greek Text.* New International Greek Testament Commentary. Grand Rapids: Eerdmans, 2005.

North, Gary. *Millennialism and Social Theory.* Tyler, TX: Institute of Christian Economics, 1990.

———. *Westminster's Confession: The Abandonment of Van Til's Legacy.* Tyler, TX: Institute of Christian Economics, 1991.

Ortlund, Dane C. "Inaugurated Glorification: Revisiting Romans 8:30." *Journal of the Evangelical Theological Society* 57:1 (March 2014) 111–33.

———. "What Does It Mean to Fall Short of the Glory of God? Romans 3:23 in Biblical-Theological Perspective." *Westminster Theological Journal* 80:1 (Spring 2018) 121–40.

Pearcey, Nancy. *Total Truth: Liberating Christianity form its Cultural Captivity.* Wheaton, IL: Crossway, 2004.

Pentecost, J. Dwight. *Things to Come.* Grand Rapids: Zondervan, 1978.

Piper, John "The Image of God: An Approach from Biblical and Systematic Theology." *Studies in Biblical Theology* 1:1 (March 1971) 15–32.

Poythress, Vern S. *The Shadows of Christ in the Law of Moses.* Phillipsburg, NJ: P&R, 1991.

———. *Understanding Dispensationalists.* 2nd ed. Phillipsburg, NJ: P&R, 1995.

Rhodes, Jonty. *Covenants Made Simple: Understanding God's Unfolding Promises to His People.* Kindle ed. Phillipsburg: P&R, 2015.

Ridderbos, Herman, N. *The Coming of the Kingdom.* Translated by H. de Jongste, edited by Raymond O. Zorn, Philadelphia: P&R, 1962.

———. *Paul and Jesus.* Translated by David H. Freeman. Philadelphia: P&R, 1958.

Riddlebarger, Kim. *A Case for Amillennialism.* 2nd. ed. Grand Rapids: Baker, 2013.

Robertson, O. Palmer. *The Christ of the Covenants.* Grand Rapids: Baker, 1980.

———. *The Israel of God: Yesterday, Today, and Tomorrow.* Phillipsburg, NJ: P&R, 2000.

Rogers, Trent. "The Great Commission as the Climax of Matthew's Mountain Scenes." *Bulletin for Biblical Research* 22:3 (Spring 2012) 383–98.

Russel, J. Stuart. *The Parousia: The New Testament Doctrine of Our Lord's Second Coming.* Grand Rapids: Baker, 1999.

Sasse, Hermann. "αἰών." In *Theological Dictionary of the New Testament*, vol. 1, edited by Gerhard Kittle and Gerhard Friedrich, translated by Geoffrey W. Bromiley. Grand Rapids: Eerdmans, 1992.

Schechter, Solomon. *Some Aspects of Rabbinic Theology.* New York: MacMillan, 1909.

Schreiner, Thomas, R. *New Testament Theology: Magnifying God in Christ.* Grand Rapids: Baker, 2008, 41.

Bibliography

Scobie, C. H. H. "The Structure of Biblical Theology." *Tyndale Bulletin* 42:2 (1992) 163–94.

Scofield, C. I. *Rightly Dividing the Word of Truth.* Edited and abridged. Danville, IL: G&T, 1996.

Stewart, Alexander E. "The Temporary Messianic Kingdom in Second Temple Judaism and the Delay of the Parousia: Psalm 110:1 and the Development of Early Christian Inaugurated Eschatology." *Journal of the Evangelical Theological Society* 59:2 (June 2016) 255–70.

Stookey, Stephen M., "Models of the Kingdom of God in Church History." *Southwestern Journal of Theology* 40:2 (Spring 1998) 38–52.

Storms, C. Samuel. *Kingdom Come: The Amillennial Alternative.* Reprinted. Fearn, Scotland: Mentor, 2015.

Stott, John R. W. *The Contemporary Church: Applying God's Word to Today's World.* Downers Grove, IL: InterVarsity, 1992.

Stott, John R. W., and Christopher J. H. Wright. *Christian Mission in the Modern World: What The Church Should Be Doing Now.* Updated and expanded. Downers Grove, IL: InterVarsity, 2015.

Strange, Alan D. *The Doctrine of the Spirituality of the Church in the Ecclesiology of Charles Hodge.* Reformed Academic Dissertations. Phillipsburg, NJ: P&R, 2017.

Symington, William. *Messiah the Prince.* Pittsburgh: Christian Statesman, 1999.

Swain, Scott R. *Trinity, Revelation, and Reading: A Theological Introduction to the Bible and Its Interpretation.* London: T. & T. Clark, 2011.

Taylor, Nicholas. "Early Christians' Expectations Concerning the Return of Jesus: From Imminent Parousia to the Millennium." *Journal of Theology for Southern Africa* 104 (July 1999) 32–43.

VanDrunen, David. "The Reformed Two Kingdoms Doctrine: An Explanation and Defense." *The Confessional Presbyterian* 8 (2012) 191–96, 286–87.

———. *Living in God's Two Kingdoms: A Biblical Vision for Christianity and Culture.* Wheaton, IL: Crossway, 2010.

———. *Politics after Christendom: Political Theology in a Fractured World.* Grand Rapids: Zondervan Academic, 2022.

VanGemeren, Willem. *The Progress of Redemption: The Story of Salvation from Creation to the New Jerusalem.* Grand Rapids: Baker, 1988.

Venema, Cornelis P. *The Promise of the Future.* Carlisle, PA: Banner of Truth Trust, 2000.

Vos, Geerhardus. *Biblical Theology: Old and New Testaments.* 11th ed. Edinburgh: Banner of Truth Trust, 2017.

———. "Eschatology of the New Testament." In *Redemptive History and Biblical Interpretation*, edited by Richard Gaffin. Phillipsburg, NJ: P&R, 1980.

———. *The Pauline Eschatology.* Reprint ed. Phillipsburg, NJ: P&R, 1994.

———. *The Teaching of Jesus Concerning the Kingdom of God and the Church.* Originally published by the American Tract Society, 1903. Eugene, OR: Wipf & Stock, 1998.

Walker, Peter W. L. *Jesus and the Holy City: New Testament Perspectives on Jerusalem.* Grand Rapids: Eerdmans, 1996.

Wallace, Daniel. *Greek Grammar beyond the Basics: Exegetical Syntax of the New Testament.* Grand Rapids: Zondervan, 1996.

Walvoord, John F. *The Millennial Kingdom.* Grand Rapids: Zondervan, 1959.

Warren, S. Goldstein. "The Dialectics of Religious Conflict: Church-Sect, Denomination and the Culture Wars. *Culture and Religion* 12:1 (March 2011) 77–99.

Watson, Thomas. *The Lord's Prayer.* 11th ed. Carlisle, PA: Banner of Truth Trust, 2015.

Bibliography

Waymeyer, Matt. *Amillennialism and the Age to Come: A Premillennial Critique of the Two-Age Model*. Woodland, TX: Kress Biblical Resources, 2016.

Wells, David F. "Our Dying Culture." In *Here We Stand: A Call from Confessing Evangelicals*. Edited by James M. Boice and Benjamin E. Sasse. Grand Rapids: Baker, 1996.

White, R. Fowler. "Agony, Irony, and Victory in Inaugurated Eschatology: Reflections on the Current Amillennial-Postmillennial Debate." *Westminster Theological Journal* 62:2 (Fall 2000) 161–76.

Wilkins, Michael J. "Original Meaning, Matthew." In *The NIV Application Commentary, New Testament*. Grand Rapids: Zondervan, 2004.

Williams, Michael D. "Theology as Witness: Reading Scripture in a New Era of Evangelical Thought." *Presbyterian* 36:2 (Fall 2010) 71–85.

Wilson, Alistair I. *When Will These Things Happen?: A Study of Jesus as Judge in Matthew 21–25*. Carlisle: Paternoster, 2004.

Witsius, Herman. *The Economy of the Covenants between God and Man: Comprehending a Complete Body of Divinity*. Translated by William Crookshank. 2 vols. Originally published 1822. Phillipsburg, NJ: P&R, 1990.

Wolterstorff, Nicholas. *Justice: Rights and Wrongs*. Princeton, NJ: Princeton University Press, 2010.

Wright, Christopher J. H. *The Mission of God: Unlocking the Bible's Grand Narrative*. Downers Grove, IL: InterVarsity, 2006.

———. *The Mission of God's People: A Biblical Theology of the Church's Mission*. Grand Rapids: Zondervan, 2010.

Wright, N. T. *Jesus and the Victory of God*. Christian Origins and the Question of God 2. Minneapolis: Fortress, 1996.

Author Index

Alexander, T. Desmond, 19, 19nn63–64, 27n100
Allison, Dale C. Jr., 50, 50n47, 104, 104n91
August, James, 74, 74n129

Bailey, J. W., 37, 37nn22–23, 41n28
Baugh, S. M., 14n47
Bavinck, Herman, 10–11, 10n33, 11nn34–37, 21, 21n69, 125, 125n148, 135n11
Beale, G. K., 15n52, 44, 45, 45nn35–36, 47n44, 48–58, 49n45, 50nn48–49, 51nn50–52, 51nn54–56, 52nn57–59, 52nn61–63, 53nn64–66, 53n69, 54nn70–73, 55n74, 56nn79–80, 57nn82–85, 58nn87–88, 64, 64nn99–100, 66–71, 66nn103–106, 67nn107–110, 68nn111–114, 69n116, 70nn118–119, 71n120, 75–77, 75n134, 76nn136–137, 77nn138–140, 91, 94, 112n117, 113, 113nn121–123, 116, 117n132, 118, 119n137, 124n144, 130n1
Beasley-Murray, George R., 21n72
Behe, Michael J., xin3
Bock, Darrell L., 15n51, 41n27
Boice, James, 102, 102n83
Bolt, John, 1–2, 1nn1–3, 2n4
Bosch, David J., 30n117, 90n39, 98, 98n63
Brow, Robert, 103n85
Brower, Kent E., 46, 46n42

Bruce, F. F., 36, 36nn16–18, 37
Bultmann, Rudolph, 24
Busenitz, Nathan, 39n25

Calvin, John, 8, 89n38, 133n6, 135n11
Carson, D. A., 45nn38–40, 46, 46n41, 57, 57n81, 60n92, 102, 102n82
Chalmers, Aaron, 9n29
Charles, R. H., 37n21
Chilton, Bruce, 21n70
Clouse, Robert G., 41n27
Clowney, Edmund, 30n116, 60, 60n90, 61–62, 61nn93–94, 62n95, 62n97, 65, 65n101, 66n102, 133n6
Cohn, Norman, 41n27
Cole, Alan, 59n89
Colson, Charles W. (Chuck), 86, 86n32, 87n34, 88n35

Dalley, Stephanie, 127n149
Danker, Frederick W., 117n131
Davies, W. D., 104, 104n91
DeYoung, Kevin, 72n121, 92, 92n50, 97, 97n61, 98n65, 105n94, 106, 106nn95–98, 107, 107n99
Dillard, R. B., 69, 70n117
Dodd, C. H., 24, 24n89, 28n102
Donaldson, Terence, 99n66, 100, 100n71, 100n73
Dryness, W. A., 49
Dunn, James D. G., 4, 5n15

Elliot, Mark W., 5, 5n16, 46, 46n42
Ellis, Peter F., 100n72
Erickson, Millard J., 2n8, 41n27

Author Index

Evans, Craig A., 28n109

Ferdinando, Keith, 105, 105n93
Frame, John, 20, 20n68, 21, 21n74, 23n85, 27n99, 27n101, 100nn74–75
France, R. T., 100, 101nn76–77, 101nn79–80, 102n81, 102n84, 103nn85–87

Gaffin, Richard, Jr., 32nn1–2, 52n60
Gage, Warren Austin, 15n53
Gamble, Richard C., 30n114
Gandhi, Mahatma (Mohandas), 84
Gentry, Kenneth L., Jr., 72n122
Gentry, Peter J., 14n47, 29n107
Gilbert, Greg, 71, 72n121, 92, 92n50, 97, 97n61, 98n65, 105n94, 106, 106nn95–98, 107, 107n99
Gladd, Benjamin L., 47n43
Goerner, Harry C., 5, 5n18
Goldstein, Warren S., 6n23
Goldsworthy, Graeme, 3n9, 14n49, 28, 28n104
Gray, John, 21n70
Green, William M., 34, 35n12
Guthrie, George H., 111, 111nn111–112, 111n114, 112n116

Harmon, Matthew S., 47n43
Hart, D. F., xiin5
Hodge, Charles, xiin5
Hoekema, Anthony A., 2n7, 17n60, 23n83, 28n100, 30n113, 33n6, 34nn7–9, 34n11, 35, 35n13, 55, 55n77
Horton, Michael, 80n3, 104, 104n92, 130n2, 131n3, 134, 134n7, 135n11
Hunter, James, 96n58

Irons, Charles Lee, 109n104, 111, 111n115

Kilner, John F., 27n100
Kline, Meredith G., 22n76, 109n104
Kolawole, Oladotum Paul, 55, 55n78
Köstenberger, J. Andreas, 79, 79n1, 80nn3–4

Kuiper, Herman, 136n11
Kuyper, Abraham, 10n33, 11n33, 98n62

Ladd, George, 2, 2nn5–6, 15, 18n31, 19n65, 21, 21n71, 23–26, 24nn86–88, 25nn90–91, 26nn93–95, 28n110, 29–30, 30nn111–112
Levison, John R., 62n96
Loisy, Alfred, 1

Manson, William, 47, 50, 51
Matthews, Kenneth A., 16, 16n55
McCartney, Dan G., 22, 22nn80–81, 23n82, 53, 53nn67–68, 108, 108nn101–102
McKenzie, J. L., 49
McNeal, Reggie, 91n42
Middleton, J. Richard, 110n109
Moltmann, Jürgen, 2n8, 17, 17n59
Moore, Geore Foot, 4n13
Muether, John R., xiin5

Neill, Stephen, 98, 98n64
Niebuhr, H. Richard, 5, 5n17, 5n19, 6, 6nn20–23, 7n24, 96, 96n59
Niehaus, Jeffery, 69, 69n115
Nolland, John, 103–4, 104n88
North, Gary, 33, 33n5, 72n122

Ortlund, Dane C., 117–19, 117n133, 118nn134–136, 119n138, 124–25, 124n146, 125n147

Pearcey, Nancy, 19, 19n62, 112, 113n119
Piper, John, 55n76
Poythress, Vern S., 132, 132n5

Rauschenbusch, Walter, 6, 89
Rhodes, Jonty, 14n47
Ridderbos, Herman N., 4, 4nn11–12, 18n31, 22, 22n75, 22nn77–79, 27, 27nn97–98, 35, 35n14
Riddlebarger, Kim, 43n31, 44, 44nn33–34, 45n37
Ritschl, A., 28n102
Rivet, 11

Author Index

Robertson, O. Palmer, 14n47, 63n98
Rogers, Trent, 99, 99nn67–70

Sasse, Hermann, 36, 36n19
Schechter, Solomon, 4, 4n14
Schreiner, Thomas R., 27n96
Schweitzer, A., 28n102
Scobie, C. H. H., 49, 49n46
Scofield, C. I., 29n106
Stewart, Alexander E., 34n10
Stookey, Stephen M., xi, xin1, xiin4
Stott, John R. W., 80–89, 80n3, 80nn5–10, 81nn1–3, 82nn4–9, 83nn10–13, 84nn14–19, 85nn20–25, 86nn26–31, 87n33, 89nn36–37, 95–97, 105, 141
Strange, Alan D., xiin5
Swain, Scott R., 3n9, 23n84, 29n108
Symington, William, 7n25

Taylor, Nicholas, xin2
Tillich, 2n8
Troeltsch, Ernst, 6n23

VanDrunen, David, 7, 7n27, 8n28, 9–10, 9n30, 12–13, 12nn41–43, 13nn44–45, 17, 17n58, 108, 108n100, 108n103, 109, 109n105, 110, 110n106, 110n110, 111, 111n113, 112, 112n116, 112n118, 113, 113n124, 115, 115nn126–127, 116, 116nn128–130, 120, 120n139, 121n140, 122, 122n141, 123n142, 124, 124n143, 135n11
VanGemeren, Willem, 3n9, 15n54, 16, 16n56, 20, 20n66

von Harnack, A., 28n102
Vos, Geerhardus, 10, 10n32, 21n70, 28, 28n103, 30n115, 41n26, 41n29, 78

Walker, Peter W. L., 57, 58n86
Wallace, Daniel, 124, 124n145
Walvoord, John F., 43n30
Warfield, 44
Watson, Thomas, 3, 3n10, 5, 7, 8, 8n28, 10n31, 13, 13n46, 17
Waymeyer, Matt, 37n20
Wells, David F., 33, 33n3
Wellum, Stephen J., 14n47
Westermann, C., 49
White, R. Fowler, 73–75, 73nn123–127, 74n128, 74n130, 75nn131–133, 75n135, 76
Wilberforce, William, 136n11
Wilkins, Michael J., 104, 104n89
Williams, C. J., 36n15
Williams, William D., 90, 90n40, 91n41, 93, 94n56
Wilson, Alistair I., 101, 101n78
Witsius, Herman, 11, 11nn38–39, 12n40
Wolterstorff, Nicholas, 25n92
Wright, Christopher J. H., 80n3, 80nn5–10, 81nn2–3, 82nn4–9, 83nn10–13, 84nn14–19, 85nn20–25, 86n26, 91–94, 91nn43–48, 92n49, 92nn51–53, 93nn54–55, 94n57, 97, 105
Wright, N. T., 60, 60n91

Zacharias, Ravi, 135n9
Zimmerli, W., 49

Scripture Index

OLD TESTAMENT

Genesis

	130	3:17–19	116
1	110, 112, 113, 115, 120	3:19	116
1:1	16	5:3	53, 109
1–2	16	8:20—9:17	9, 115, 119
1–3	41	8:21	12
1:5	110	8:22	12, 13
1:8	110	9	118n136
1:10	110	9:6	118n136
1:26	109, 115	9:9	12
1:26–26	111	9:10	12
1:26–27	109	9:13	12
1:26–28	54, 55, 111n112, 112, 123, 130n1	9:15	12
		9:16	12
1:28	54, 110, 115, 130n1	9:17	12
2	18n61, 19, 112, 113, 115, 120	11:3–4	119
		12	29
2:1–3	111	12:1–3	54, 102
2:7	61	15:6	15
2:9	112	18:16–33	135
2:15	20, 55, 112, 116, 123	22:18	22
2:15–17	112	39:5	135
2:16–17	115	45:4–8	82
2:19–20	55	47:27	54
2:22	55	48:3–4	54
3	73, 114, 115, 116	49:1	50
3:5	114	49:8–12	50
3:6	115	49:10	22
3:14–19	73		
3:15	9n29, 14n50, 22, 29, 74, 74n129, 115, 119, 120	### Exodus	
		1:7	54
3:16	116	3:10	83

Scripture Index

(Exodus continued)
19:8	68
20:22	68
24:15–18	68

Leviticus

	64, 65
26:11–12	65

Numbers

11	70
11:1—12:8	70
11:11	70
11:16–17	70
11:17	70
11:24–25	70
11:25	70
11:29–30	70
23:10–11	54
24:14–19	50

Deuteronomy

4:36	68

2 Samuel

7:12–14	22

2 Chronicles

20:30	25n92
36:22	25n92

Ezra

1:1	25n92

Nehemiah

9:35	25n92

Esther

1:14	25n92
1:20	25n92
3:6	25n92
3:8	25n92

Psalms

2	99
2:12	129, 133
8	111
8:5–8	111n112
18:3	69
19:1	117, 119
29:7	69
103:13	21
103:19	3, 9
145:11–13	21n73

Isaiah

	69
2	69
2:2	69
2:2–4	50
2:3	69
4:2–6	66n106
5:25–25	69
9:6–7	132
24:5	23n85
30	69
30:27–30	66n106, 68, 69
42	99
56:3–8	60
57	64
57:19	63, 64n99

Jeremiah

3:16–17	66n106
7:25	83
7:26	83

Ezekiel

	64, 65
36	57
36:25–27	57
37	57
37:26–27	65
37:26b	65
37:27	65
38:14–16ff	50
38:14–17ff	50
40–46	66n106

Daniel

	100
1:20	25n92
2:19–20	110
2:28–45	50
7:13	100n73
7:13–14	100, 101
7:13f	100
7:14	100
9:1	25n92
10:14—12:10	50
10:14ff	50
11:2	25n92
11:27—12:10	50
11:27–35	50
11:30—12:3ff	51
11:40–45	50
12:1–13	50
12:2	50

Hosea

3:4–5	50, 50–51

Joel

2	69, 70
2:28–29	69

Micah

4:1–3	50

Haggai

2:9	59

Zechariah

1:16—2:13	66n106

NEW TESTAMENT

Matthew

	66, 98, 100, 105, 106
1:1–17	101
2	101
4:1–11	120
4:8–9	115
4:8–10	100
4:17	104
4:18–22	104
5:1	104
5–7	98
6:10	24
7:11	90n38
9:2–6	59
9:3	59
10:5–6	101
11:4–6	48
11:11	18n61
12:6	59
12:28	26
12:32	38, 41
13	20
13:24–30	42
13:36–43	42
13:39–40	43
13:40	38
13:41	20, 101
13:49–50	43
16	71

Scripture Index

(Matthew continued)

16:8	100
16:16–18	71
16:19	71, 131
16:28	101
17	98
18	71
18:15–20	131
19:28	101
20:21	101
21:1–11	101
21:12–13	60
21:31	18n61
23:13	18n61
24	99, 101
24:3	38
24:9	102
24:14	102
24:30	102
25:31–32	43
25:31–34	101
25:32	102
25:34–36	140
25:37	140
25:40	140
27:11	101
27:29	101
27:37	101
27:42	101
28	2n4
28:16–20	83, 98, 105
28:18	100, 101, 102
28:18–20	100, 100n73, 142
28:18b	99, 100
28:19	105
28:19–20	101
28:19–20a	99, 102
28:20	38, 104, 130
28:20b	100

Mark

	41, 66, 83, 105n94
1:11	99
3:29	41
6:6	86
10:15	24
10:21	117n131
10:29–30	41
10:30	38, 42
10:32	41
10:45	84
11:15–19	60
13:10	105
14:9	105
16:15	83, 105n94

Luke

	66, 105, 106
7:28	18n61
7:49–50	59
11:52	18n61
16:8	38, 42
16:16	18n61
18:17	24
18:30	39
19:12	24
19:15	24
19:45–48	60
20:27–40	42
20:34	41
20:34–36	39, 41, 48
22:20	15
22:29–30	132
23:42	24
24:44–49	83, 105
24:46–51	57
24:47	105
24:50	68

John

	56, 66
1:16	131
1:29	60
2:19–22	59
3:1–15	57
3:3	57
3:5	57
3:15	57
5:24	57
5:24–29	57
9:22	137

13:34–35	140	8:30	124n144
14:26–27	106	10:17	131
16:33	106	12:1–2	142
17	139	12:2	14, 14n48, 39, 42
17:18	83	12:5	62, 65n101
17:20–23	138	15:25–26	137
17:21	139	16:25	36
18:3	24		
18:36	3		
20:21	83, 106		

1 Corinthians

1:20	39
2:6	39, 42
2:8	39
4:8–11	46
7:14	135
8:1–7	136
10:11	42–43
10:18–22	131
12:27	62, 65n101
14:21–22	69
15	108, 121, 122
15:20	122
15:21	122
15:35–37	43
15:45	61
16	136

Acts

	106
1	57
1:1	79
1:1–11	57
1:6	3, 57
1:8	83, 105, 106
1:11–12	68
1:14	68
2	58, 66, 67, 69, 70
2:1–2	68
2:1–12	69
2:2	68
2:22–36	58
2:24	58
2:30–31	58
2:33	70
2:42–47	138
6	85, 88
6:1–4	136
10:38	86
13	58
13:33	58
24:17	137

2 Corinthians

3:18	65
4:4	39, 41, 42
5:14–17	52
5:17	52, 123
6	65
6:16	59, 64, 65
6:16b	65

Romans

3:23	116, 117, 118, 119
4	15
5	108, 121
5:12	118
5:12–19	112, 121
5:15	121
5:16	121
8:29–30	124, 125

Galatians

1:4	36, 40, 41, 42
3:11	15
6	64
6:15	52, 63
6:16	63

Ephesians

1:10	15
1:21	40
1:21–23	13
1:22	17, 32n2, 108
2	63, 64
2:2	40, 42
2:3	64
2:4–7	123
2:6	132
2:9	48
2:17	63
2:19–22	63, 64
2:20–22	61
2:21	62, 65n101
3:10	71
4:12	62, 65n101
4:16	62, 65n101
4:24	109

Philippians

4:18	62n97

Colossians

1:13	18n61
1:15–18	52
2:15	120
3:10	109

1 Timothy

2:14	114
6:17–19	40

2 Timothy

1:9	36

Titus

1:2	36
2:12	40
2:13	40

Hebrews

	111, 122, 123
1:3	9, 121
2	121, 122
2:4	123
2:5	111, 114, 123
2:5–8	111, 122, 126, 129
2:8	114, 122
2:9	48, 122
2:9–10	124
2:14	120
4:1–10	111
4:4	124
4:9	124
4:10	123
4:12–14	131
4:14	123
4:14–16	121
4:15	122
5:10	123
6:4–6	47
6:5	40
7:1	123
7:1–28	123
7:23–28	121
7:26	123
8:1–2	123
9:11–28	121, 123
9:26	42
10:12	123
10:13–13	132
10:19–22	121

1 Peter

	9n29

2 Peter

3:3	104
3:3–15	43
3:13	36

1 John

2:17	42

3:17–18	85	5:6	75, 76
4:9	84	5:9	16, 19, 75
4:10	84	7:9	16
4:14	84	10:6	19n65
		11:15	20, 53
		12:9	114
		18	120

Revelation

1:5	52, 76, 77	20:10	120
1:5–6	74, 76	20:14–15	120
1:6	75	21:1–3	16
1:9	76, 77, 123, 129, 133	21:1—22:5	77
2–3	75	21:4	19
2:10–11	77	21–22	16
3:14	52	21:22	20
4:3	11–12	22:2	112
5:5	75	22:4–5	19–20
5:5–10	75	22:5	53

www.ingramcontent.com/pod-product-compliance
Lightning Source LLC
Chambersburg PA
CBHW072136160426
43197CB00012B/2136